SUPPORTING THE CITY

SUPPORTING THE CITY

the influence of engineering on Glasgow's buildings

edited by
Howard Wright

WHITTLES PUBLISHING

Southern approaches to the Clyde Tunnel

Published by:
Whittles Publishing
Roseleigh House, Latheronwheel, Caithness KW5 6DW

© Howard Wright

ISBN 1-870325-97-4

Design by Janet Jamieson

Printed by Interprint Ltd., Malta

Contents

Foreword

ALF YOUNG, Deputy Editor, The Herald

The last year of this millennium, the year in which Scotland reconvened its first parliament since 1707, is a good time to reflect on what this small country has achieved to date and could yet achieve in the years ahead. No part of Scotland should feel left out of that worthwhile scrutiny. While Edinburgh adjusts to its role as home of the Scottish Parliament once more, its great rival Glasgow may feel that the limelight has, temporarily, deserted it. But 1999 also brought to Scotland's most populous city the accolade of UK City of Architecture and Design, a unique opportunity to celebrate the best in Glasgow's built environment, the legacy of the countless generations who have shaped and reshaped the dear green place into the vibrant city we know today.

Glasgow may still look a bit battered and scarred as it emerges from the massive industrial, technological and social changes of the twentieth century. Most of its manufacturing capacity has gone. Many of its people have left for new towns, suburbia or the New World. Glasgow has made the at times painful journey to a fresh raison d'être, as a major service, retail and leisure hub. Glasgow is still smiling but there is certainly plenty of unfinished business confronting the city and those who would deign to run it. But there also, as inspiration, are the great central cityscapes and vital services like the water supply and the Underground bequeathed by the enterprise and skills of our Victorian forebears. And there too are a growing number of modern structures, from the Armadillo to Hampden Park, from the SECC to Buchanan Galleries, all of which bear witness to the fact that, as far as Glasgow is concerned, enterprise did not begin and end with the Victorians.

This book is, first and foremost, a celebration of Glasgow's physical landscape, of how generations of Glaswegians have taken nature's topological and geological legacy at this particular point where the Kelvin meets the Clyde, and built a city that can both delight the eye and set the spirits soaring. As a journalist, my whole business is words. Words build into stories. But the contributors to this book know intimately the very different and acutely daunting challenges which come when you build with stone and brick, concrete, glass and steel. In *Supporting the City* they bring to their various commissions not just brimful enthusiasm but also vast experience and expertise.

When the First Minister spoke at the formal opening of the new Scottish Parliament and tried to define who we Scots are, among the images Donald Dewar evoked was that of the welder shouting in the din of the great Clyde shipyards. Some argued later that he focused too much on the role of skilled labour and too little on the contribution of the naval architects and design engineers without whom there would have been no Scottish shipbuilding industry. There is a similar danger in celebrating Glasgow's structural evolution solely through the designs in stone and steel left imprinted on its physical face by generations of gifted architects. The great structures that support any city owe just as much to those professional engineers whose challenge it is to turn great designs into great and enduring structures.

Scotland owes much to its rich engineering heritage. That debt is not always adequately reflected in the esteem in which we hold our engineering profession. This book is not just about some of the great buildings and structures, old and new, which make Glasgow the city it is. It is also about the engineers whose sustained problem solving and technical inspiration have made that evolution possible. I salute them and their many achievements. I hope that, as you read on, you will join me in toasting those whose skills and talents, quite literally, continue to support and underpin this great city, Glasgow.

LIST OF CONTRIBUTORS

Professor Howard Wright
Head of Department
Department of Civil Engineering
University of Strathclyde
107 Rottenrow
Glasgow, G4 0NG

Dr. Sam Thorburn OBE
Consultant
32 Lochbroom Drive
NEWTON MEARNS
Glasgow G77 5PF

Mr. John C.M. Allen
Ground Engineering Manager
Glasgow City Council
231 George Street
Glasgow, G1 1RX

Mr. Jim Shipway
Consulting Civil and Structural Engineer
1 Belgrave Road
Edinburgh, EH12 6NG

Mr. Arthur Bryan
Senior Partner
McLay Collier and Partners
7 Park Circus Place
Glasgow, G3 6AH

Mr. W.J. Stuart
Consultant
Old Manse
Well Road
KILBARCHAN
Renfrewshire. PA10 2LZ

Mr. Neil Buchanan
Buchanan (CE) Limited
Consulting Engineers
1 Lubnaig Gardens
Bearsden
Glasgow, G61 4QX

Mr. W.M. Reid
Director
Thorburn Colquhoun
243 West George Street
Glasgow, G2 4QS

Professor Iain MacLeod
Professor of Structural Engineering
Department of Civil Engineering
University of Strathclyde
John Anderson Building
107 Rottenrow
Glasgow, G4 0NG

Mr. Jim Hampson
Chairman
Ove Arup & Partners Scotland
Scotstoun House
South Queensferry
West Lothian. EH30 9SE

Mr. Lawson Clark
Director
Thorburn Colquhoun
243 West George Street
Glasgow, G2 4QE

Mr. Robert Wilson
Chartered Structural Engineer
Kirklands
16 St. Margaret's Road
North Berwick
East Lothian. EH39 4PJ

Introduction

HOWARD WRIGHT

The number and variety of buildings in Glasgow are a testament to over 600 years of continuous development. From the earliest surviving building, the Provand's Lordship (Figure 1) to the most recent landmark the 'Armadillo' (Figure 2) all have required the involvement of engineering knowledge and skills.

Prior to the mid-1800s such engineering input was only clearly identifiable in the large churches and the Cathedral (Figure 3). Very special skills and abilities were needed to conceive an appropriate geometry, to commit this to drawings and then to supervise the workforce during construction. In addition the financing of such structures involved the master builder in raising money, purchasing materials and paying for the work done.

Smaller structures were built by builders with skills passed on from father to son. They needed less ability to conceptualise new solutions as they were generally reproducing structures that they had previously built or seen built before.

FIGURE 1
The Provand's
Lordship.

However in both cases it is easy to underestimate the level of ability possessed by builders of the day. No one can fail to be impressed by the height of the nave in Glasgow Cathedral or by the longevity of the Provand's Lordship.

In the late 1700s the Industrial Revolution began to change the way of life for so many people. It was a time of new ideas and unprecedented activity. In Glasgow, as elsewhere, there was a migration of workers, from the country and into the cities, in order to find work in the new industries. In Glasgow's case shipbuilding was the primary industry. As the empire grew the need for freight and passenger transport increased and the River Clyde proved an excellent waterway upon which to base this industry.

It was fortuitous that coal and iron ore were found locally and that the workforce could easily adapt to working in the new wonder material of iron and later steel. Glasgow's reputation as a producer of quality ships grew quickly and the motto 'Clydebuilt' became a watchword for excellence.

The next chapter of this book provides a more detailed history of Glasgow and the brief note regarding the inception and growth of shipbuilding is used here only to provide a background to a description of the transfer of talent and ideas from the manufacturing industries to building industries.

The industrial revolution was fuelled by an exponential rise in technological innovation which dragged social change with it. The technological and social changes affected construction also. Initially the existing technology was used and developed to cater for the increasing requirements of manufacturers for workshops, mills and warehouses and for the large numbers of new houses needed for the workers in the shipyards and factories. The Glasgow tenement house is a well-known type of building that satisfied this need. However the use of iron and steel and powered machines in the manufacturing industry soon crossed to the building industry. Iron was first used for columns and beams in

FIGURE 3
Glasgow Cathedral.

the warehouse buildings and lifts developed in America in the late 1800s allowed taller buildings to be constructed. Until the advent of the mechanical lift, six storeys was considered the most people could be expected to climb. Even at this height the weight of the building was such that the first storey masonry walls had to be made so large that only very small windows could be included. The use of steel columns replaced the mass of the masonry walls allowing a more usable first floor space. Steel frames and lifts were innovations that made the skyscraper in America possible and this technology has been copied for many of Glasgow's buildings such as the warehouses on Jamaica Street (Figure 4).

The new technology required the masons and builders of the time to adapt quickly. However, often the engineering input came from the new specialists and entrepreneurs. Key exponents of iron and steel building components were often the foundry owners themselves looking for markets for the new material. Whilst the new materials were stronger, lighter and less expensive than the

FIGURE 4
The application
of innovative
engineering in
Glasgow's Jamaica
Street warehouse.

traditional materials they demanded a different approach to design and construction. In addition there was no tradition associated with them and their limits were often not fully appreciated. The well-known Tay bridge disaster in 1879 was caused by a lack of understanding of the brittle nature of iron.

Steelwork and lift machinery were prefabricated and required detailed drawings to be made of the construction. The components were much more slender than traditional materials and clients required proof that the new elements would be safe and satisfactory in service before they would agree to their use. Consequently 'engineering' became a more essential part of building as the 1800s progressed. Engineering skills were also different to those previously used by masons and builders in construction. The 'engineer' had to design a structural solution and then validate that it would carry the applied loads safely and satisfactorily for an appropriate period of time before work began. Such validation could be provided by testing the whole construction but was more conveniently carried out by using mathematical models to extrapolate the behaviour of small, easily-tested components. Consequently construction changed from being a largely one stage craft-based operation to one demanding high levels of intellect with a design and construct phase.

Prior to the industrial revolution the aesthetic look of buildings had been formed over a long and gradual development of style, largely associated with decoration. For example the style of churches in the 12th century was dominated by the Roman arch which gradually changed over the following centuries to the high Gothic pointed arch prevalent in the 1800s. The new materials provided huge potential for the building form to change although the natural conservatism of most clients initially led to only minor changes in building form.

It must also be remembered that prior to the Industrial Revolution most large buildings were constructed by a close team of builders who combined aesthetic and structural considerations quite naturally in their skills. The new technologists had little classical training in architectural form and in any case the complexity of the engineering satisfied their intellectual demands. This led to the construction of structures being identified with two professions, the architect looking after the form and aesthetics and the engineer looking after the structure and construction. It is the author's view that this split was an unfortunate turn of events that has only recently been partly resolved by the creation of design teams on recent projects.

The Industrial Revolution is often regarded as a specific and finite period of British or world history. However in practice it should be regarded as a turning point in technological and social development. Whilst steel was, perhaps, the most important single material associated with the period subsequently developments in concrete, ceramics and composites have continued to provide new inputs to a rapidly-changing building industry.

Of these, concrete is, perhaps, the material that has resulted in the greatest change due to its use in the construction of the buildings in which we live and work. Chapter 5 describes the Lion Chambers which is one of the first reinforced concrete buildings in Britain and certainly the first in Glasgow. Whilst almost a hundred years on it is suffering problems, partly due to neglect, it should be remembered that at the turn of the century this was a very new material and technology. Developments in the use of concrete led to the boom in industrialised housing during the sixties described in Chapter 9. The problems associated with this era of construction were as much to do with the imposition of social changes in living as with the technology of construction and they highlight the need for engineers and politicians to work more closely together.

The Industrial Revolution provided improvements in the construction of buildings and in the living conditions of the more wealthy. Houses were more effectively insulated and draught-proofed and amenities such as public baths, concert venues and transport structures were constructed. The engineering is most advanced in this range of buildings and this book details several examples. Sports structures and especially football stadiums, for example, are major landmarks on the cityscape of Glasgow and are, arguably, some of its most frequented buildings. Chapter 8 describes the engineering thought processes that go into these structures which now form one of the most technically-demanding design exercises for structural engineers.

That is not to say that other public structures are undemanding. Consider Glasgow's latest landmark the 'Armadillo'. Chapter 10 shows that the integration of structure, architecture, acoustics, and building environment has led to an innovative and integrated solution to the client's requirements. Working as a team is now the watchword for modern engineering.

Along with the increase in urban populations during the Industrial Revolution came the need for a more developed infrastructure. Glasgow boasts one of the very first underground systems and it is a tribute to the engineers of the day that its construction and means of propulsion were both innovative and unique. Chapter 4 details the development of the system and whilst it is not strictly a building its impact on the buildings of Glasgow warrants its inclusion in this book.

With virtually all of the buildings and structures described in this book, a major problem to be overcome was how to ensure that the ground would support the design. Chapter 3 describes the geology and resulting soil profiles in the Glasgow area. It also provides an insight into the problems associated with building on a river valley and how engineers have overcome these problems. However over recent years there has been an increasing demand to re-use land in the city centre. Such land may be desirable either due to its city centre location or because it is cheap. The Scottish Exhibition and Conference Centre was constructed as a part of the Garden Festival in 1988. It was built on a large area of old dockland that had to be filled and compacted. Chapter 7 is concerned with the reclamation of the dock area and this theme is picked up in Chapter 11 which describes some of the latest office buildings in the Broomielaw area. This development is at the forefront of structural technology using the latest composite systems that integrate component parts of the building to provide economy, in material costs and construction time.

But what of the future? Recent stand-alone structures such as the Armadillo are clearly icons to the future but even in this case considerable thought has been put into ensuring that the ecology and environment is not affected unduly. The building is built on reclaimed land and is energy efficient. Other experiments with energy-efficient buildings have been common over the last

FIGURE 5
Strathclyde
University Halls
of Residence.

few years as demonstrated by Strathclyde University Halls of Residence on George Street (Figure 5). However, both the aesthetics and the environment are increasingly seen as worth preserving and many of Glasgow's newer buildings have been built within existing façades. Modification of the existing façade is generally more demanding on the engineer than construction on green-field sites. This can possibly be envisaged when examining the temporary bracing required to hold a Victorian façade on Ingram Street (Figure 6).

The main purpose of this book is to celebrate the architecture and design that is so individual to Glasgow. However a secondary purpose is to explain the input of engineers to our built environment. Perhaps also it is possible that this book may inspire younger readers to enter a career in engineering and to take part in the shaping of the city in which we live and work.

The idea for this book was hatched at a meeting with Sam Thorburn and Neil Buchanan in 1997. Both Sam and Neil are contributors. Sam, in particular, has provided unbounded encouragement throughout its production. I would like to thank Sam, Neil and all the other contributors who have made this book possible.

FIGURE 6
Victorian façade
in Ingram Street.

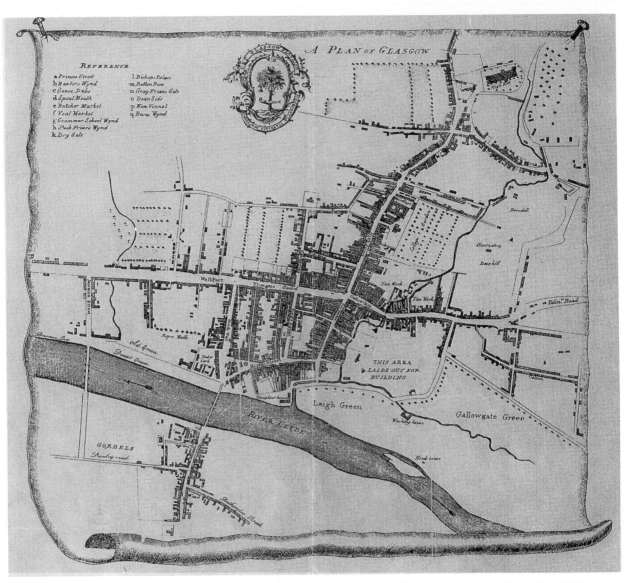

A plan of Glasgow from Ross' map of the Shire of Lanark, published in 1773. The strips of land, founded on the Viking 'rigg' system can be seen. The width of these riggs related to the space required to turn an ox and cart (or plough). (Courtesy Glasgow City Archives).

Matters of
Historical Interest

SAM THORBURN

Much has been written about the origins and development of the City of Glasgow, and the Mitchell Library retains many valuable and interesting publications which portray the great history of this most ancient city.

The ancient landscape within the Glasgow district is essentially pre-glacial and was formed during a period when the land surface was at an elevation at least 90 m higher than today. Although the ancient primary drainage system is similar in direction to the existing system, the contours of the ancient land surface within the district indicate that two large valleys exist along the axes of synclinal folds. These two large valleys in the pre-glacial landscape had been infilled with alluvium before glaciation and ice-movement sculptured the district. The pre-glacial valleys converge at Clydebank and Renfrew, and the River Kelvin flows for a considerable distance along the axis of the deepest buried valley, known as the Bearsden or Kelvin channel (Figure 1).

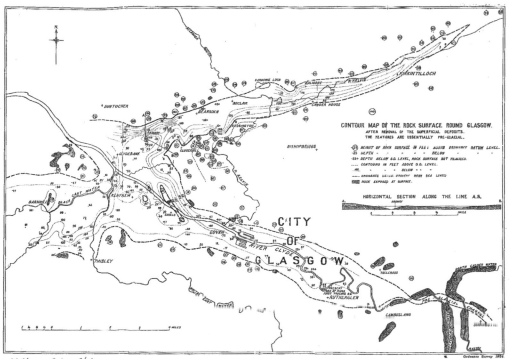

FIGURE 1
Contour map of the rock surface around Glasgow.

The main drainage channel of the district at the present time is the River Clyde, and it is of interest to note that the course of the river is coincident with the axis of the shallower of the two buried valleys.

The central portion of Glasgow is mainly situated on the relatively flat plain which exists on either side of the River Clyde. On the north side of the river, the ground surface slopes steeply upwards from the perimeter of the alluvial plain, and the northern portion of the city is underlain by glacial till.

Civilisation first embraced the inhabitants of the Glasgow district about 80 AD.

Agricola, the Roman governor of Britain, 78-84 AD, advanced into Scotland about 80 AD and penetrated as far north as Perth. A fort was built at Inchtuthil (near Dunkeld) to hold 5,500 men. There were barracks and administration offices, a drill hall and officers' quarters, a hospital and a large workshop. Fortresses like this were rare in Britain and not numerous elsewhere in the world. The Roman Empire only had 27 legions, so there could never be more than 27 fortresses fully manned by complete legions (this major unit of the ancient Roman army consisted of 3,000 to 6,000 infantry troops and 100 to 200 cavalry-men).

Trouble flared in Europe and the legion at Perth was recalled with haste by Rome about 86 AD. The Romans did not wish to leave anything which could be fashioned into weapons by the warlike Picts. The soldiers dug a pit in the corner of the large workshop, poured about 900,000 nails into the deep hole, packed two metres of soil on top, and then carefully demolished the building to remove all traces of their activities. The pit and its contents remained undiscovered for nearly 1,900 years, and so the Romans achieved their objective of preventing the Picts from obtaining a unique and large source of material for weapons.

Urbicus, the Roman governor of Britain after Agricola, built a wall across Scotland about 142 AD. The wall was 37 miles long, with small forts positioned at two-mile intervals, such as the one at Kirkintilloch. Three legions (2nd, 6th and 20th) were engaged in the construction of the wall which was named in honour of the then Roman Emperor, Antoninus Pius. The wall was positioned a few miles north of Springburn and was built to confine the barbarous Picts (called Caledonians by the Romans) to the land north of the wall.

About 181 AD the Romans withdrew south to the protection of Hadrian's Wall and left the people of Glasgow to continue a simple rural existence. The early Glasgow dwellers had enjoyed 100 years of Roman patronage and protection and 370 years passed before the next historically important event took place, with the advent of St Kentigern about 550 AD.

Accounts of the life of St Kentigern are vague and wrapped in legend. However, as far as we can ascertain from the fragments of knowledge available, he was born in Culross, Fife, about 530 AD. Kentigern was the son of Eugenius, third King of Scotland and Thametis, daughter of Lothus, King of Picts and was educated and trained as a priest of the Celtic Church by St Serf at the Culross Monastery. The name Kentigern means High Lord and St Serf called him Mungo, meaning my dear friend. After finishing his training about 550 AD, Kentigern intended to spend some time with a holy man, Fergus, but soon after they met Fergus died. Kentigern decided, for some unknown reason, to convey and bury the body of Fergus in the west of Scotland – perhaps Fergus was born in the west.

He subsequently travelled to Glasgow and established a church within an area of green hills overlooking a crystal clear river, now known as the River Clyde. It was on the banks of the Molindinar watercourse, which is the outlet from Hogganfield Loch, and which flowed into the River Clyde, that St Kentigern had his residence. It was here that he was visited by St Columba and where he founded his church within the 'beloved green place' (Glasgu), hallowed by this visit. The church building may have been similar to the simple structures of wood combining church and cell favoured by St Columba and built in Ireland.

St Columba presented St Kentigern with a crook of simple wood on the occasion of his visit to Glasgu. St Kentigern was a man of rare piety and, to the poor, exceedingly generous. It is recorded in ancient writing that he wore a shirt of coarse hair cloth and over that a garment made of the skin of goats and a close hood covering his head. His pastoral crook was always in his hand and he carried with him a manual for spiritual guidance in his travels.

Kentigern lived an ascetic and holy life until his death. He died on 13 January 603 AD, was canonised and became the patron saint of Glasgow.

It was approximately 500 years later, in 1175 AD, before the next historically important event occurred, when Bishop Jocelyn was placed in charge of the church in Glasgow.

Bishop Jocelyn, formerly Abbot of the Cistercian monastery of Melrose, had taught King David, youngest son of Malcolm Canmore and Queen Margaret. He was granted the right to form a Burgh of Regality by William the Lion, sometime between 1175 and 1178 AD, and to hold a fair in 1189 AD for eight days from 6 July (Glasgow Fair fortnight is 810 years old).

Glasgow was unlike other burghs in that the common lands were held, not from the Crown or from a baron, but from the bishop, and as their feudal overlord the bishop exercised domination over the people, particularly in the matter of local government affairs. He appointed the magistrates and controlled their actions. The burgesses annually had to submit to him a list from which he selected those whom he desired to act as magistrates. The city was simply a bishop's burgh (technically a Burgh of Barony) ruled by ecclesiastical authority. Even after it had been raised in 1450 to the status of full regality by a charter of King James II, no advantage accrued to the citizens; it simply meant an improvement in the dignity of the bishop. It may be noted, however, that the first provost was appointed in 1472, probably as the result of the raising of the city to the rank of a Burgh of Regality.

Under the feudal system, the title baron was applied to all who held land direct from the Crown. They were sometimes called lesser barons to distinguish them from peers, and they all were obliged to attend Parliament. The barons had a jurisdiction conferred on them in both criminal and civil matters, the extent of which was governed by a royal charter.

In raising a Burgh of Barony to the rank of a Burgh of Regality, the King thereby conferred the highest feudal dignity and the greatest powers which it was possible for the sovereign to depute to a subject. The Lord of Regality and the magistrates of the burgh, in addition to all the rights of a barony, had a jurisdiction over all the residents within the Regality.

FIGURE 2
Ladywell Street
and Cathedral,
circa 1849.

In Burghs of Barony or Regality, the magistrates and members of council were in some cases appointed by the Baron or Lord of Regality; in other cases they were elected by the burgesses, subject to the approval of the feudal lord.

In creating Royal Burghs, the King desired to have a class of freemen between himself and the powerful barons; burgesses who held land directly from the King himself. They would owe no allegiance whatever to any feudal lord and were under obligation as King's Burgesses of doing service to the King only. In Royal Burghs, the burgesses elected the magistrates.

Glasgow was elevated to a Royal Burgh in 1611 by James VI, and this improvement in rank and privilege was confirmed in 1636 under a charter of King Charles I. The lands and privileges were thereafter held directly from the sovereign and the *burgh maill* was paid to the treasury instead of, as formerly, to the bishop, in respect of these privileges. After the Reformation the right to nominate and control the magistrates was claimed and exercised by the Protestant archbishops or other feudal lords who had succeeded to the temporalities, with the result that Glasgow burgesses had not the independence enjoyed by the burgesses in other Royal Burghs. Indeed, the adjoining Royal Burghs of Rutherglen, Renfrew and Dumbarton had a superior status to that of Glasgow, although the city was much more progressive and enterprising.

Not until 1690 can the city be said to have become free. Under a charter of William and Mary in that year, complete control in choosing their own magistrates and other officers for the management of the city was granted unreservedly (as in all other Royal Burghs) to the free inhabitants of Glasgow.

In the 12th century, magistrates held their meetings in Bishop Jocelyn's castle. About the 15th century, they moved their meetings to premises at Glasgow Cross, known as the Tolbooth. The original Tolbooth building became dilapidated and was rebuilt in 1626, including the existing tower which is a remnant of the 1626 building.

A sketch plan of the City of Glasgow in the 16th century, originally published in Volume I of *Glasgow Protocols, 1530–1600*, (see Figure 4), shows the site of Glasgow Cathedral and of the Church of St Kentigern.

Glasgow Cathedral is the oldest building in the city, construction having commenced in the late 12th century and largely completed by the end of the 15th century. It was constructed on the ground above the Molindinar Burn, which is now essentially culverted and flows underground to the River Clyde. Hogganfield Loch is the source of the Molindinar Burn. Gardens and orchards existed to the south and west of the Cathedral, within which existed the dwellings of the clergy. The only evidence of the buildings of this medieval community is the Provand's Lordship.

The motto of the City of Glasgow was inscribed on the bell of the Tron Church, cast in 1631.

Lord let Glasgow flourish through the preaching of thy word and praising thy name.

The arms of the City of Glasgow show a *Tree*, with a *Bird* perched in its boughs; on one side a *Salmon* with a *Ring* in its mouth; and on the other a *Bell*.

The salmon and the ring are the emblems of the miraculous recovery of the love-pledge of the Queen of Cadzow. The legend tells of the Queen of Cadzow,

FIGURE 3
The Fiddler's Close,
17th century.

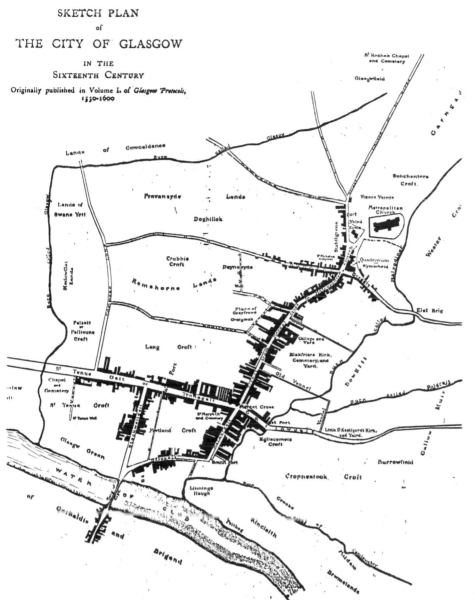

SKETCH PLAN
of
THE CITY OF GLASGOW
IN THE
SIXTEENTH CENTURY
Originally published in Volume I. of *Glasgow Protocols,*
1530-1600

FIGURE 4
Sketch plan of The
City of Glasgow in
the 16th century.

who was suspected by her husband, King Roderick, of being intimate with a knight whom he had asked to hunt with him. When the knight was asleep, the King removed from his satchel a ring given to him by Queen Cadzow. In furious jealousy, King Roderick threw it into the Clyde. After the day's hunting they returned to the palace at Cadzow, and in the course of the evening the King asked the Queen where her ring was. It could not be produced. Death was threatened if it were not forthcoming. The Queen sent one of her maids to the knight for the ring and, being unsuccessful, a bearer was sent to St Kentigern making a full confession of the affair.

The saint sent one of his monks to the River Clyde, instructing him to bring home alive the first fish he caught with his fishing rod. This was done. St Kentigern found the ring in the mouth of a salmon, and speedily sent it to the Queen, who restored it to her husband, thereby saving her life.

The scene of the legend is well-represented on the annexed counter seal of Bishop Robert Wysechard.

The tree is a token of a miracle which St Kentigern wrought at Culross when the lamps of the monastery were extinguished. He tore a frozen bough from a neighbouring hazel and, making the sign of the cross over it, it instantly kindled into flame. This legend constitutes the third lection for the Saint's day.

The bird represents a tame robin, the favourite of St Serf, which was accidentally killed and torn to pieces by his disciples at Culross, but was miraculously brought to life again by St Kentigern.

The bell commemorates a famous bell which was brought from Rome by St Kentigern, and preserved at Glasgow until the Reformation, if not, indeed, to a more recent period. It was called St Mungo's Bell, and was tolled through the city to warn the inhabitants to pray for the repose of the departed soul.

All these tokens appear first in the seals of the Bishops of Glasgow in the 12th and 13th centuries, from which they were transferred to the common seal of the City, at the beginning of the 14th century. *[Pref : Liber Collegii Nostre Dominie Glasguensis].*

The history of Glasgow is long and varied and significant events are listed below:

- Roman influence : 80 to 181
- Influence of Church of Rome: 1175-1611
- Great Plague: 1649
- Great Fire : 1652
  Population 13,000 in 1700
- Tobacco and sugar trading : 1707-1780
- Cotton and steam: 1780-1830
  Population 100,000 in 1800
- Chemical works, railways, heavy engineering and shipbuilding developed 1830-1870
  Population 500,000 in 1870
- Marine and locomotive engineering developed: 1870-1930

The Industrial Revolution altered radically the nature of business in the City of Glasgow. By the beginning of the 19th century there were established numerous diverse manufacturing industries, including iron and engineering, pottery and glass, chemical and tar, dye and paper works.

In large industrial cities, extensive areas of land surface are artificial and have resulted from the deposition of a wide variety of materials derived from industrial processes to elevate low-lying ground and to backfill old stone quarries and clay pits. Glasgow is not an exception. Ancient watercourses have been culverted and now exist as buried features. All such historical hidden features may remain unknown until exposed by the unwary.

The St Rollox chemical works was built at Sighthill in 1799 by Charles Tennant and became the largest of its kind in Europe. These works were demolished about 1965, leaving a physical legacy of massive deposits of chemical waste within the district.

The development of such a major chemical facility at the end of the 18th century originated from the need of the bleaching industry to cope with the

FIGURE 5
The Molendinar
Burn, circa 1883.

output from the cloth industry, whose efficiency of production had been greatly increased by the introduction of weaving machinery. In 1785, Berthollet read a paper before the French Academy, presenting his attempts to expedite the process of bleaching cloth using chlorine gas. His proposals proved impractical as a commercial solution since control could not be exercised over this diffusive and noxious gas which made the process intolerable to the workers bleaching the cloth.

Lime had been used as a bleaching agent, but its use was forbidden by an Act of Parliament because it destroyed vegetable fibre. Charles Tennant discovered that lime had a great affinity for chlorine gas and manufactured a solution of chloride of lime in 1788. In 1799, he patented a method of producing a dry compound of lime and chlorine, and this powder completely revolutionised the process of bleaching cloth. The success of the large chemical works resulted from this innovative process. The powder was made by passing the chlorine gas over large trays of slaked lime (calcium hydroxide produced by the action of water on calcium oxide) and the process produced large quantities of alkaline waste. The advantages accrued from this discovery were dramatic and the bleachers were able to work safely and economically, with their former monthly output becoming their daily output.

The process was later modified to achieve greater production, and manganese, sulphuric acid, hydrochloric acid, potash, lime and magnesia were used. The rate of accumulation of the by-products of the process became serious, and in 1803 the matter was temporarily resolved by the production of an impure soda from the residue. Recovery of the manganese from the residue took place after 1855.

The location of the works within the City of Glasgow, and the massive deposits of the solid residue which accumulated during the long period of chemical production presented a major problem. Care was taken to deposit and compact the chemical waste such that it was as impervious to rainwater as possible. However, the carbonic acid in rainwater caused chemical changes within the waste, and some compounds being soluble in water were dissolved and leached (taken out in solution) by the rainwater. The chemicals in solution then entered the local watercourses.

As the works expanded, the volume of noxious and muriatic (chlorine) fumes increased. Although several tall chimneys had been built to convey the poisonous fumes to remote and uninhabited areas, people continued to complain of the tainted air. It was these chimneys that gave the grandson of Charles Tennant the idea of building the tallest chimney in existence to release the fumes even higher in the atmosphere and reduce their effect. The chimney concept was developed by Professor W.J. McQuorn Rankine and was designed by Professor L.D. Gordon and L. Hill. Dugald Campbell McIntyre, once foreman bricklayer at St Rollox, and by then a private contractor, built the chimney.

On 29 June 1841, the concrete foundations of the chimney were laid 6 metres below the surface on sound sandstone rock, and exactly a year later the coping stones were laid, 133 metres above ground surface. The chimney was 15 metres in diameter at the base, tapering to 4.42 metres at the top, and took five months to complete. To alleviate the nuisance caused by smoke from the

FIGURE 6
The Gorbals
Steeple, 1845.

works, tunnels were formed through the sandstone rock from various furnaces towards the 133 metres high chimney with one large main tunnel receiving the branches and linking them to the chimney. For 80 years, until its demolition in the 1920s, 'Tennant's stalk' was a landmark, and enjoyed national and international fame (Figure 7).

As the chemical works expanded, immense and increasing quantities of odorous wastes spoiled the land and polluted the streams. By the 1860s the chemical waste was said to cover about 80 acres and, according to the Alkali Report 1883, 'There were nearly 100 acres of crude calcium sulphide constituting a vast grey desert, a mass of 3,000,000 tons in some places, 24 metres thick'. Bog waters and springs took some of the waste into the Pinkston Burn, thence into the River Kelvin and, finally, into the River Clyde. In the channel of the River Kelvin the sulphide of calcium liquors from St Rollox met the waste of other factories, especially acid from the distilleries, and produced obnoxious fumes of hydrogen sulphide.

Drainage was considered to be the answer, and a shaft was driven about 15 metres down into the sandstone rock below the huge mound of chemical waste and tunnels were formed in various directions. Pumping was continued night and day for years. The problem remained intractable, and in 1864 the company laid a 225 mm pipe all the way to the River Clyde. This gave rise to a new problem. Ship owners complained that the copper sheathing on the hulls of their ships was corroding as a result of the chemical pollution of the River Clyde. In 1871, James McTear, the manager at St Rollox and a chemist, partially solved the problem of pollution by inventing a process of sulphur recovery. This beneficial and profitable process relieved temporarily the situation, but the waste was a constant liability and a cause of public complaint.

To complete this historical account, mention must be made of some of the features of the city which are notable. A building of historical importance is the Merchants' House. When the Lanark County buildings were constructed in Wilson Street, the Merchants' House occupied a hall in the new building. The original Merchants' House was built in Bridgegate in 1659. This building was demolished in the early part of the 19th century, but the steeple was preserved and placed under the care and maintenance of Glasgow town council. The weather vane on the steeple was a gilded ship, the symbol of the

FIGURE 7
The 'Tennant's stalk' chimney.

Merchants' House. Property at the north-west corner of George Square was built in 1877 to accommodate Merchants' House, and the weather vane on the building continues to symbolise the history of the city.

The city centre of Glasgow has a system of streets essentially based on a square pattern, aligned north-south and east-west. The modern street system may have developed from that formed in the 16th century, and shown on the sketch plan (Figure 4).

When the first Jamaica Bridge opened in 1768, the city extended as far as Buchanan Street and Jamaica Street, although most people lived in the older parts of the city from the Saltmarket and eastwards along the Gallowgate.

The first square was developed in 1768 and formed around St Andrew's Church. St Enoch's Square was planned to complete Buchanan Street. George Square was developed in 1786. The stage of development of the city at the end of the 20th century is shown in Figure 8.

An interesting account of the radical, and perhaps destructive changes to the historical City of Glasgow is described in Frank Worsdall's book, *The City that Disappeared*. However, it is not the purpose of this author to criticise past decisions, but rather to interest young and old in the history of the city.

The population of the City of Glasgow is about 700,000 and the city has the enviable record of being the largest shopping centre in Scotland. Service industries such as banking, finance, insurance and retailing now form the core of the economy of the city and the thrust of the creation of opportunities for work.

The infrastructure and buildings required to accommodate organisations responsible for education, health, sport, recreation, administration and courts of justice, together with the need for commercial provisions, have created a modern city of unique identity.

REFERENCES

1 Gordon, J.F.S. (Ed.) *Glasghu Facies*. James Duncan, Gibson's Wynd, Saltmarket, 1736.
2 McNaughton, J. A *Glasgow Vade-Mecum*, 1947.
3 MacGeorge, A. *An Inquiry as to the Armorial Insignia of the City of Glasgow*. Private circulation, 1866.
4 Worsdall, Frank. *The City that Disappeared*. Richard Drew Publishing, 1981.

FIGURE 8
An aerial view of the city.

The Royal Technical College

The Royal Technical College was the 'Largest Building in the Kingdom devoted to Education' at the time of opening in 1910. In June 1964 it became the main building of the University of Strathclyde. Photograph provided by the University of Strathclyde.

The University of Strathclyde, John Anderson Building, 107 Rottenrow, Glasgow, G4 ONG

Foundations to a City, and Beyond

JOHN C.M. ALLEN

FOREWORD

On account of the fact that there is no glory in the foundations, and that the sources of success or failure are hidden deep in the ground, building foundations have always been treated as stepchildren – and their acts of revenge for lack of attention can be very embarrassing'.

Karl Terzaghi, Building Research Congress, London 1951.

Buildings may be admired for generations yet their foundations are seldom considered. In researching the foundations of Glasgow it became apparent that in the post-war era, Glasgow (and Scotland) has benefited from the expertise of many gifted geotechnical specialists, too numerous to mention individually, but a few of whom have contributed internationally to the art and science of ground engineering. The influence of these engineers is seldom recognised beyond their specialist branch of engineering, but their work forms the foundations of modern Glasgow and is part of the most recent chapter of Glasgow's architectural heritage.

INTRODUCTION

Glasgow was once known as the Second City of the Empire. As an important commercial centre it had expanded rapidly after the Industrial Revolution to become a vibrant industrial conurbation. It is recognised as an excellent example of a Victorian city and large parts are now protected in conservation areas. The early history of the city is uncertain, and compared to other similar townships, its development appears unusual. Glasgow had a 'defensive hill site' and was a route centre lying at the highest ford of the River Clyde. The city did not develop until medieval times. When rapid development did occur modern Glasgow was founded on ground which varied in type, origin and engineering characteristics and included areas of very difficult foundation conditions.

It is believed that an early Celtic monastery was constructed on the defensive site of Glasgow Cathedral and that the tomb of St Kentigern (more commonly known as Mungo) lay on the steep eastern slope running down to the Molendinar burn. In the 12th century, when it was decided to build the Cathedral it was stipulated that St Mungo's tomb should be within the building. In order to keep the Saint's grave within the Cathedral an extraordinary piece of underpinning (the creation of foundations beneath or within an existing building) had to be constructed directly below the choir to provide a platform at the same level as the nave to the west. Unique to Glasgow Cathedral and sometimes described as a crypt, this underbuilding is more properly an under or lower church and has been described as one of the greatest architectural treasures of the medieval period in Scotland. Construction of the cathedral is thought to have been carried out in several phases but it is essentially the 13th century cathedral which substantially survives today, including the underbuilding.

By the middle ages Glasgow comprised two communities or towns, the high town consisted of an ecclesiastical centre located around the Cathedral and nearby necropolis, and the low town lay on the flood plain of the river Clyde and its tributaries. This was a vibrant, bustling township which had developed from the high town to become an important commercial centre with trade links to the New World. It extended along the northern banks of the Clyde from the haughlands of the Camlachie and Molendinar Burns in the east to the Glasgow Burn in the west. The area included the High, Low and Calton Greens (now known simply as the Glasgow Green), Little Green and Greenhead (where Stockwell Street now lies) and the original Glasgow Green now occupied in part by St Enoch's Square.

Little is known about the building methods used to construct the low town. It is thought that early construction comprised mud and stone walls or possibly timber. Four storey tenemental properties were built in 1591 and 1596 at Trongate and the High Street and, although thought to be exceptional before the great fires of 1652 and 1677, this type of development set a pattern of housing which extended through Victorian times and up to the First World War.

As Glasgow prospered, the rectangular pattern of development of the present city centre was laid out and built to the west of the old town. Very shortly, a similar pattern of development followed south of the river but here the ground conditions were much poorer. Trade, commerce and the wealthier people moved westwards, upwind of the overcrowded and poorly-ventilated old town, whereas the poor moved south of the river into Gorbals and Hutchesontown; names that survive to the present day associated with poor housing conditions.

Another important but often forgotten factor that contributed to the original rapid growth was the Declaration of Independence by the American Colonies. Glasgow's trade and commerce suffered severely but this blow contributed to the birth and growth of the Industrial Revolution. Glasgow had wealth, world-wide trade connections, raw materials and a cheap workforce and the merchants and city fathers invested their finances in new industrial ventures to replace the lost trade. Raw materials such as coal, fireclay, limestone and ironstone were mined locally and engineering and manufacturing industries developed. Goods manufactured in Glasgow and the surrounding towns were exported throughout the world and again Glasgow flourished.

GEOMORPHOLOGY AND GROUND CONDITIONS

Glasgow is bounded by hills to north and south which comprise mainly volcanic rock, rounded and denuded after the passage of successive ice sheets.

These strong rocks provided a degree of protection to the softer sedimentary rocks and subsequent processes of erosion and deposition produced superficial deposits (unconsolidated materials usually brought into the area by natural agencies, and relatively young in geological terms) which created the landforms of today. Deposition of glacial debris laid down and compacted during a series of glacial incursions was interspersed and followed by the deposition of soils under estuarine conditions when the sea was much higher than at present. In turn alluvial materials (products of rivers and streams) and former deep river channel areas affected by erosion have infilled.

The glacial depositional cycles resulted in a swarm of mound-like elongated hills, or drumlins, stretched out in the direction of the ice flows. These features have been likened to a basket of eggs when seen from the air.

Geographically, the early low town of Glasgow was situated at a fording point on the flood plain of the River Clyde. Many of the nearby towns also developed from settlements along the banks of the rivers Clyde, Cart and Kelvin, and other burns and they too would also contribute to the growth of the city. These early settlements were sited mainly on deposits of alluvial origin, materials with widely differing engineering properties. The freshwater alluvium comprises granular soils of varying compaction, extensive soft clays and silts, sometimes containing pockets of compressible organic soils. Marine alluvial deposits were similar but in general contained less organic materials. The development of the city encountered glacial drumlins and areas of shallow rock, often associated with areas of poor drainage.

The Central Belt of Scotland comprises mainly sedimentary rocks, heavily faulted and folded, with numerous igneous intrusions. The sedimentary rocks fall within the Old Red Sandstone and Carboniferous Periods. Volcanic rocks (lavas) are also found, for example at Castlemilk.

On these varied deposits the present city of Glasgow was founded.

EARLY FOUNDATIONS AND METHODS OF GROUND TREATMENT

The cathedral is founded primarily on glacial till (sediments laid down by glacial ice) but little is known of the early foundations to the remainder of the town. However, the expansion of the medieval city encroached upon areas which even today cause problems to the foundation engineer.

Around 1345 an eight-arched masonry bridge was built across the River Clyde to replace the earlier timber bridge at the ford crossing. This new structure survived some 400 years and at the southern end of the bridge the small village of Gorbals was established. This village subsequently became a focal point around which the city expanded south of the river in the early 19th century.

Beyond the area of the established old town, Glasgow developed as a series of new towns. The upstream sections of the Clyde were rapidly becoming unnavigable to larger ships and river traffic was confined to small craft, mainly for fishing or carrying timber. To enable trade and commerce to develop further the town council founded Port Glasgow some twenty miles to the west, on the Clyde estuary. Land for the port was purchased in 1668, the port opened in 1676 but the town was not laid out until 1690. However, it soon became apparent that major and ongoing river improvement schemes were necessary. This resulted in interesting and innovative methods of foundation engineering and land reclamation that were forerunners to ground engineering techniques of today.

An ambitious project to dam the river and construct locks at Marlin Ford (near Partick) was proposed to enable shipping to reach Glasgow. Work commenced in the spring of 1760 and continued through the summer months until winter when the cold, the darkness and almost continuous flooding made work impossible. After clearance of the winter flood debris, construction work resumed with the construction of the masonry walls for the locks. Unfortunately, the underlying soft alluvial soils could not support the heavy loadings of the high walls for the locks and foundation failures occurred. The scouring and siltation from the spring floods of 1762 exacerbated the problems and, despite strenuous efforts to raise more capital, the scheme was formally abandoned later that year.

However, the cause was not abandoned and by 1772 the river had been dredged to allow a clear depth of five feet (1.5 m) which by the early 19th century had been increased to ten feet (3 m). The river had originally been directed between jetties and dykes which reduced the effective channel width and increased the ability of the river to scour a channel. Parallel walls were created between the jetties and dykes, further increasing the scouring ability of the river. Obstructions such as hard dense materials which resisted the scouring effects were broken up using a plough-like tool which was dragged across the river bed. Quays were constructed, further dredging carried out, and larger and larger shipping accommodated. By 1885 ships with a twenty-five foot draft could sail into Glasgow and at the outbreak of the Great War the depth had been increased to thirty feet. In 1936 the great liner *Queen Mary* with a draft of thirty-five feet (10.7 m) was launched.

Materials dredged were dumped behind retaining walls and in this way intertidal marshes and sandbanks were reclaimed releasing new land which would subsequently prove ideal for development. With the advent of steam engines, marine engineering flourished and these large flat sites, together with the improved river channel, contributed to the Clyde becoming a shipbuilding centre of world importance. Shipbuilding developed west of Glasgow, took housing westwards and supporting trades flourished everywhere. Unlike contemporary ports such as London and Hull, which developed inland from the waterway, Glasgow's harbour facilities extended linearly along the Clyde towards the shipyards.

The river containment works incorporated the construction of some massive retaining structures. Many of the earlier quay walls comprised a row of sheet piles in front of a timber frame which was built on timber bearing piles and tied back to an anchorage formed with more piles driven some distance to the rear of the wall. As the depth of the river increased the construction of the quay walls was adapted to support masonry walls founded on bearing piles. This construction method proved satisfactory and enabled walls to be erected on a wide variety of soil conditions, even where earlier foundation failures had occurred. The volume of trade and the size of the shipping continued to increase and additional dock capacity was constructed inland, usually parallel to the river. The first inland dock was built behind the Windmillcroft Quay on the south bank and later became known as the Kingston Dock. The next major off-river basin created was at Stobcross where the dock walls were supported on concrete piles sunk by grabbing and weighting, a process similar to that adopted in sinking shafts whereby the outer shell is constructed while a vertical shaft is sunk and the spoil removed. The outer shell would ultimately be infilled with concrete to form a large pile or caisson.

The next major dock to be constructed was at Cessnock which comprised three parallel basins opening off a canting basin at the western end. The dock was completed in 1897 and was known as Prince's Dock.

The use of such piling methods illustrates familiarity with advanced piling techniques. Surprisingly, little evidence remains to indicate that piled foundations were used to support Victorian tenements located on poor ground. Nor would it appear that many of the large commercial properties were founded on piles.

Initially, little development had taken place outwith the old bridge end village of Gorbals. Between 1768 and 1772 a bridge, known as the New Bridge, was constructed to the west of the town. By 1814 the area known as Trades Town had been built, the Glasgow to Ardrossan Canal constructed towards Johnstone and the area of Laurieston laid out for development. All these areas were located upon very weak alluvial soils, mainly on strip footings (ribbon-shaped foundations for walls) or in a very few instances strip footings incorporating means of articulation. It is worth recording that the third bridge crossing of the River Clyde, the almost-completed Hutchesontown Bridge, was swept away during severe flooding in November, 1794 and was replaced by a timber bridge (1803) and subsequently a stone bridge (1829-34).

Riverside locations were exploited for housing and so Carlton Place, 'composed of houses on the first rank, in point of architectural beauty', took full advantage of the Clyde's south bank. It was recently discovered, during the restoration of Laurieston House at Carlton Place (originally built around 1804), that the house was supported on an unusual foundation system comprising masonry strip footings interrupted with and incorporating timber. The foundation system was devised to reduce the effect of differential settlement. This magnificent house also contained an upper floor which was suspended from timber rafters by wrought iron tie rods. Effectively the upper floor was free to float within the main building as the loadings transferred from the roofing level through the external walls to the foundations. In an area of such poor ground conditions this represented an unexpected appreciation of the likelihood of differential settlement. Other instances of timber being incorporated into strip foundations or foundations placed on a timber grillage have been encountered in areas where excessive settlements could have occurred. Usually very little timber remains but damage directly attributed to foundations being placed on timber or comprising timber appears to be rare. The concept of constructing flexible buildings on foundations able to tolerate movements is not new and has been used with considerable success, even in areas of very poor conditions.

The high density housing of the old Gorbals, Laurieston and Hutcheson-town areas comprised traditional tenemental buildings. It seems that the

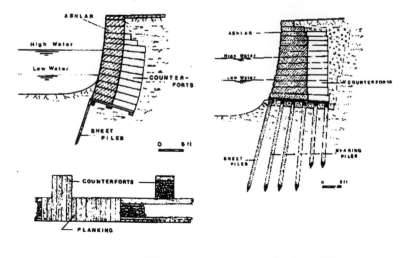

a) circa 1810s   b) circa 1840s

FIGURE 1 (a), (b), (c) AND (d).
Glasgow made the Clyde and not the River Clyde made Glasgow. After the
foundation failure of the locks at Marlin Ford (near Partick), when the ambitious
project to dam the river was eventually abandoned, quay structures beside the
deepened river became increasingly massive. Initially sheet piles helped
provide passive resistance against circular or rotational failure and provide a
factor of safety against shear forces. As the wall heights increased loadings
were transferred to deeper horizons by bearing piles which would also develop
skin friction along their length. Ultimately lateral resistance by anchor lines and
tie rods would be added. Figure a) is typical of the structures built when the
river was initially deepened and figures b) to d) indicate the development of
the structure to the 1870s when the river was approximately 6m in depth.
(courtesy of J. F. Riddell and John Donald Publishers Ltd).

majority of these buildings were founded on nothing more than strip
foundations located in the upper crust of the soils or within a thin layer of fill.
Demolition of those old buildings revealed that the foundations often
comprised masonry blocks with little or no cement between, thus allowing
some movement to occur. Despite the simplicity of the foundations these
buildings remained structurally serviceable for many generations and were
often demolished for social reasons or because the buildings had not been
adequately maintained rather than the results of foundation failure. Elsewhere
along the River Clyde very rapid expansion during the Industrial Revolution
led to new industries being surrounded by tenemental properties, built to
provide housing for the work forces. Again these buildings were founded on a
variety of ground conditions ranging from the extensive deposits of alluvium
adjacent to the river to heavily overconsolidated glacial tills.

The expansion of the old town towards the rectilinear development of the
city centre as it is laid out today was then underway and continued as the developments south of the river mushroomed. The north bank of the Clyde had
been developed and the village of Grahamston, located approximately where
Anderston lies today, engulfed. Blythswood New Town was built to the west of
the old town, on the rising ground of a glacial drumlin. Buildings extended
southwards to meet the riverside developments and then northwards where

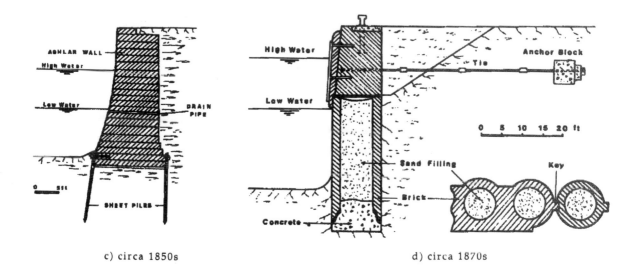

c) circa 1850s

d) circa 1870s

the drumlin at Garnethill was also being built on. The glacial till of the drumlins provided an excellent founding material and soon there were town houses at Park Circus and Park Terrace overlooking the area now occupied by Kelvingrove Park, the Art Galleries, and the Kelvin Hall. Glasgow University was relocated from the original 15th century site east of the High Street to the drumlin west of Kelvingrove Park and the magnificent University buildings enjoy a panoramic vista southwards to the River Clyde.

The hills of the drumlin swarm have been incorporated into all phases of subsequent developments. Many major cemeteries are located on these features, especially on the steep north-facing slopes which receive relatively little sunlight, as are large parks such as Bellahouston and Queens. Multi-storey buildings, such as Moss Heights, were founded on the stiff glacial till of a drumlin. Latterly council housing estates spread over the surrounding areas and extend partially or completely over drumlins. Benefit was often derived by constructing water towers at the crests of the drumlins enabling a gravity water supply to be provided for the surrounding developments. However, the low-lying areas between the drumlins often contained poor soils with bad drainage and very few appreciate how these hollows were utilised to great advantage as the Industrial Revolution gathered momentum.

The rapid growth of industry depended on the availability of suitable raw materials. The Forth and Clyde Canal and the Glasgow Branch Canal (and others) were opened and, by the late 18th century, these canals linked Glasgow to the ports of the River Forth as well as connecting with local sources of raw materials in Lanarkshire and beyond. Glasgow received ocean-going shipping, bringing in raw materials including textiles and tobacco and exported a wide range of goods to Europe. The canals followed land contours, rising slowly at locks, and travelled along the sides of hills. The slopes often bordered areas of poor drainage and these were infilled to provide large raised platforms, level with the canals, which created suitable sites for industries which thrived in the 19th century. Large steelworks and ancillary industries grew rapidly. Ash was a major waste product of the manufacturing processes and its disposal

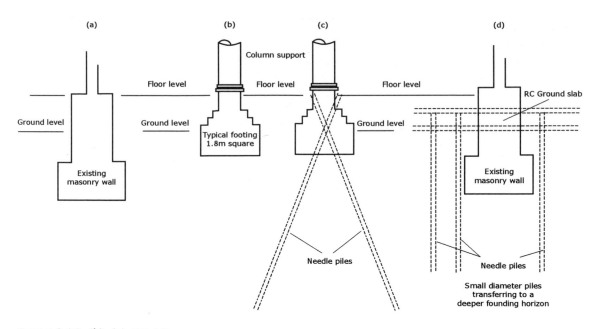

FIGURE 2 (a), (b), (c) AND (d).
Many of Glasgow's outstanding sandstone buildings are founded on simple strip and pad foundations a) and b). To avoid differential settlements occurring during redevelopment of the Victorian buildings, such footings are often supported by small diameter needle or stitch piling, c). In cases of severe distress it has sometimes been necessary to provide a ground slab incorporating piles d) to transfer additional loadings to deeper founding horizons. Where façades have been retained and the building interior constructed behind the façade loadings are transferred to horizons capable of supporting the foundation loadings and ensure very low differential settlements occur.

was in turn utilised to infill more areas and provide further sites to enable industrial development and expansion to continue. The difficulties of building on poor natural soils were overcome, the difficulties of carrying out major industrial processes on hilly terrain were negated and transportation of materials and goods made much easier. One example of such reclamation and site preparation was at Springburn and Cowlairs and the areas surrounding the famous St Rollox and Atlas works. Here the Reids, Nielsons and Dubbs, later to become the famous North British Locomotive Works, and the Caledonian Railway Works, built railway engines many of which would be exported throughout the Empire and beyond. The reclaimed areas also encompassed the Sighthill Railway Goods Yard, the St Rollox (coal and mineral) Depot, several iron and steel works to the east and St Rollox Chemical Works to the west. The area continued westwards towards the Forth and Clyde Canal which formed the western and southern boundary to the platform. It is perhaps ironic that the canal, which was in itself a superb engineering feat, should have been used to transport raw materials to establish the major engineering and railway works that would subsequently provide the next generation of transportation.

Other examples are at Parkhead, Tollcross and Cambuslang. The successful development of major industries at all these locations suggests that a degree of control must have been used when the infilling was placed. After the subsequent demise of these major works and the demolition of the buildings, the sites are being utilised again to support the next cycle of development. St Rollox is being redeveloped as a commercial area and the successful Cambuslang Investment Park is situated at the site of a former major steel works.

Perhaps one of the largest infilling exercises carried out in Victorian times was the infilling of the western banks of the River Kelvin to the north of Kelvinbridge. Here the bridge crossing is at a level approximately twenty metres above the River Kelvin. The road westwards from St George's Cross towards the Kelvin is generally flat and west of the bridge a large drumlin at Dowanhill was cut into thus reducing the severity of the road gradients. This roadway, Great Western Road, formed the western approach to the city and the original tenements east of the river Kelvin and the magnificent town housing west of Byres Road still survive today. A road was constructed to the north, along what is now Belmont Street, to a second bridge crossing of the Kelvin known as the Belmont Street Bridge. This bridge and road joined the higher ground of North Kelvin with Great Western Road and the whole of the area forming the flood plain west of the Kelvin was infilled. It is thought that a road network comprising Colebrooke Street, Colebrooke Place and Belmont Street was constructed first and the remaining areas were infilled later. Materials nearest the road were probably placed from the road side then the internal areas infilled and raised. Unfortunately the method of infilling was not controlled as for the industrial developments and the fill appears to have been in a relatively unconsolidated state when building began. Dramatic differential movements have occurred which can still be seen on properties surviving today. Differential settlements of the order of 250 mm have been measured between the front and rear walls and the buildings lean to the rear, suggesting that the fresher infilling was tipped to the rear, further from the roads. Some original buildings of this area were built upon a raft of timber foundations and, as at Laurieston House at Carlton Place, the use of timber within the foundations is attributed with helping to reduce the effects of settlements.

THE EFFECTS OF MINING AND QUARRYING ON THE FOUNDATIONS OF GLASGOW

The continuing wealth of Glasgow and the advancement of industry in the 19th and early 20th centuries occurred because of the local availability of the essential raw materials. The bedrock within the Central Belt of Scotland is heavily faulted and folded and the extraction of the economic minerals is difficult in comparison to other more uniform areas of Britain. Nevertheless, mining in Scotland was extremely successful and the former Royal College of Science and Technology (now Strathclyde University) achieved international recognition as a training establishment for mining engineers. Early records from both Culross and Paisley Abbeys record the working of coal in the 12th and 13th centuries. However, very few records survive relating to mining before the late 19th century.

Coal, iron and limestone were all worked extensively to provide materials for the iron and steel industries and cementstones were also worked locally. In some areas fireclays were worked and the overlying coal removed at the same time because it formed an unsafe roof material. The extensive library of coal working records suggest that coal was the material most worked. Many forget that ceramics were produced locally and exported world-wide. Armitage Shanks of Barrhead and Howie at Hurlford, near Kilmarnock, are two world famous names associated with ceramic goods. Below is a comparison of costs of economic materials from 1804-5:

Description	Price	Converted Price
1 cu. yd. of good sandstone	1 shilling	5 p
1 ton Airdrie Blackbird Ironstone	2 shillings	10 p
1 ton limestone	6 d	2½p
1 ton coal	5 d	2 p
1 ton fireclay	5 – 40 shillings depending on purity	25 p – £2

The cost of fireclay was 12 to 100 times that of coal. Sometimes the foundation engineer of today overlooks the relative values of the minerals extracted.

The legacies of such vigorous extraction of the sub-surface economic materials are often not obvious at ground surface. Abandoned mineshafts can present difficulties to development as instability can result in spectacular movements causing structural damage and public risk. Movements associated with the collapse of abandoned shallow workings can and do cause serious damage to buildings. Abandoned quarries and brick pits have often been built over, sometimes resulting in damage due to poorly-compacted infilling. In one particular case in Hillhead, a brick pit preceded a sandstone quarry from which coal horizons were worked from the quarry face. Elsewhere in the city major underground headings (hand-driven tunnels) were driven from the face of major sandstone quarries. Such quarries were often used as dumps but it is not known if the headings were infilled.

The greatest potential hazard causing damage to buildings or risk to people was perceived to be movements associated with past shallow mining or mineshafts. Such movements are not uncommon but it is important to keep the magnitude of this problem in perspective. Current practice dictates that construction does not take place over abandoned mineshafts as collapse can result in severe or catastrophic local damage. Unfortunately our forefathers did not abide by such rules and mineshafts were frequently built over. It is not certain whether these early builders were aware of past mining activities, which may have ceased long before new developments, or whether other criteria contributed to building over such hazards.

Many methods of infilling shafts were adopted including:

- infilling the shaft completely, often with the waste materials from an adjacent shaft or working;
- bridging at the highest level worked or at rockhead and backfilling;
- cutting down a green leafy tree hoping that it will snag at as high a level as possible and thus require a minimum of backfilling;
- putting railway tracks, railway wagons or large timbers in the shaft to snag the shaft linings, again at as high a level as possible and backfilling;
- capping or bridging near ground level and backfilling.

Experience shows that it is usually the cheapest method of infilling the top of the shaft that was used. Unfortunately timber rots with time, a weak arch of the fill materials remains and collapse can occur. Tenements and other buildings have been built over such shafts but there are many instances where a change of the building line has coincided with the likely position of an abandoned shaft, suggesting some degree of knowledge of these potential hazards. It is also not uncommon for areas of tenemental properties to merge into two-storey terraced housing and for the tenements to be just clear of the outcrop zone (i.e. where it shows at the surface) of a seam worked at shallow depth, again suggesting some degree of local knowledge.

A similar problem to abandoned shafts, but generally of a lesser risk, is potential damage above shallow workings in the outcrop zone. The magnitude of the risk and extent of resulting damage depend on a number of factors including the thickness of the worked horizon, depth of overlying strata, nature of the overburden materials, type of structure involved and whether water is available. The likely thickness of any worked seam should always be taken into account. Less obvious is the nature of the floor of the workings. The floor could comprise fireclay which was economically viable. Roadways were required for transporting the worked mineral to the bottom of the shaft and these were often larger than the workings. The nature of the overlying strata is also important. Glacial till will act as a soft rock and the effect of any disturbance will be local or absorbed while at other extreme, saturated loose sands or silts can flow into voids in an apparently random fashion thereby exacerbating the effect of failure. As with the majority of all ground engineering failures the presence of water is an important factor. It is often water from ruptured services that has caused severe damage, by washing away materials from below foundations, rather than the original collapse

FIGURE 3
An abandoned mine shaft collapse.

mechanism on its own. This fundamental and simple understanding of the effect of water in geotechnical engineering and foundation failures is not always appreciated.

The majority of shallow workings were mined using partial extraction methods whereby rock is left *in situ* to provide support to the overlying strata, However, a variety of worked conditions have been encountered ranging from the traditional stoop and room to areas where large rooms were created and roof support provided by propping. The Knightswood Gas Coal was extensively worked throughout much of the city and has often been associated with a high risk of instability. In some parts of the city, however, workings are known to be relatively limited, comprising small tunnels leading into scant areas of working. Significant damage has also occurred to properties because of movements even though the cover to the worked strata was considered too thick for significant surface movements to take place. In a few seams the workings do not appear typical of traditional stoop and room workings, but consist of large rooms, approximately 25 metres by 35 metres. Often the roof supports have deteriorated causing movements that are now reflected at ground surface. Such problems were encountered during the mineral consolidation programme to infill mineworkings below tenemental properties

The building type is also an important factor when considering risk analysis; for example, a single-storey, flexible, industrial building is much less at risk of serious damage than a four-storey tenement where the only means of access and escape is the common stairway. Fortunately the number of incidents annually within the UK relating to mineral subsidence is small.

FIGURE 4
Old mine workings.

As Glasgow grew, the building stone was taken from numerous quarries of many different sizes. The large quarries are well documented but very often small quarries served a local area and were subsequently infilled and built upon

FIGURE 5
A mine working roof supported by timber props.

almost immediately. There are many signs that buildings were settling while construction took place, extra courses of brickwork appear between floor level and windows, stringer courses fall towards the areas of maximum settlements while the eaves are comparatively level, and internally the fall of the floors was so great that care had to be taken to ensure the castors below heavy pianos and tables were lying at different directions! Even when severe damage has been repaired and the buildings underpinned by transferring the loadings to the quarry floor using bored cast *in situ* piles or mini piles, unusually large drops on the floors remain. This is because the existing building fabric and method of construction above ground level remain in place.

Many of the tenements built over old quarries and the adjacent quarry edges were founded on traditional strip footings. The areas affected by the most severe damage occur where the building straddles the original ground (where little settlement occurs) and the adjacent areas where the self-weight of the infill ing and the superimposed building loads can result in spectacular differential movements. Behind the Episcopal Church of St. Mary's Cathedral on Great Western Road lies Holyrood Quadrant. Here some account had to be taken of the former quarry underlying part of the site and a massive raft was laid to support the block of tenements. Settlements have still resulted but these are of more acceptable magnitudes than would otherwise have been the case. Such precautionary methods were rare and in most instances the builders relied on the inherent flexibility of the tenemental structure to accommodate movements.

Similar problems have occurred at the site of former brick pits. However, although both quarries and brick pits were sometimes infilled with waste materials serious chemical contamination has been encountered at the former massive brick pits near Shawfield Stadium where chromium waste was dumped. Many of these sites have been built over, often for commercial purposes, capped by car parking and this has been regarded as a satisfactory usage of such sites. Movements that have occurred can be considered cosmetic and flexible structures have tolerated large movements. Large buildings using massive foundations have also remained serviceable. However, the problem of seriously contaminated soils reaches beyond the area of the former brick pits and much more stringent criteria apply for housing, both for the foundations and public safety.

Within another area of former quarries a local contamination of radon gas had been recorded. Although not serious in itself it typifies the range of contaminants from former chemical works, gas works production, heavy industry and the wide spectrum of other industries which were present throughout Glasgow.

THE POST-VICTORIAN ERA

As the Victorian city flourished so did the surrounding towns. High-density housing and small to medium industrial works, often supporting the major industries, proliferated resulting in a densely-populated industrial conurbation. Glasgow's boundaries expanded, swallowing up the towns of Govan and Partick. Early masonry four-storey tenemental properties had been constructed in the 16th century in what must have been gap sites. By Victorian times the tradition of the Glasgow tenement was already well-established whereby a relatively strong but flexible masonry building was built on shallow strip footings. Sometimes large building settlements had occurred and occasionally measures to improve articulation of the building were included at foundation level. Both these factors suggest that the early builders could accommodate significant differential settlements. Two 'rules of thumb' for these earlier builders are undoubtedly based on experience which, with the benefit of modern knowledge, were very reasonable guides for foundation construction in areas of poor ground conditions. The first was that if a foundation bearing pressure of ½ ton/square foot (50 kN/m²) was not exceeded then foundation failure or excessive differential movements were unlikely to damage tenemental properties badly, although significant settle-ments may occur. The second rule was that if the weight of soil excavated for the foundations was equivalent to the weight of the structure proposed then the buildings would perform satisfactorily. This is the reason why many tenements in areas of poor soil conditions were built with basements. Many major structures like Central Station and the original Lewis's building were effectively constructed using this principle which is equivalent to utilising today's concept of buoyant raft foundations.

The foundations relating to the eight bridges which cross the river, the tunnels for the subway, the former tunnel below the river at Finnieston and the tunnels for the major rail routes are all worthy of separate chapters as engineering feats. Many of these projects have required foundations laid below the water table or tunnels driven through saturated soils. The importance of road, rail and the former canal routes to Glasgow cannot be underestimated and the associated structures have survived very heavy usage. However, of particular relevance was the undoubted ability of the Glaswegian foundation engineer to construct foundations and to tunnel in adverse ground conditions.

The city underwent little large-scale alteration between the Victorian era and the depression. The next significant phase of Glasgow's development comprised the building of peripheral housing estates and industrial estates. The latter were often located over areas of poor ground, for example at the infilled clay pits at Shawfield and Rutherglen and on the weak alluvial soils at Hillington. Flexible structures and associated car parking located over the chromium waste materials in the clay pits of Rutherglen effectively encapsulated the contaminated ground. The industrial estates generally included one and two-storey buildings designed for a variety of uses. On sites such as Hillington the ground conditions varied dramatically over very short distances, ranging from compact sand and gravel to very soft silts and clays. Even for one and two-storey structures, differential settlements could be excessive and thus a variety of foundation systems were employed. Single-storey buildings were founded on layered infilling, effectively preloading the soils and reducing the effects of settlement. Two-storey buildings might be piled to sound strata, constructed on strong raft foundations or with very substantial ground beams.

An unusual problem which has been encountered while building in areas of very soft alluvium is that layers of saturated weak materials have permitted the transmission of vibrations resulting in excessive movements being experienced elsewhere. Although rare there are recorded instances of structural damage occurring more than half a mile from the original source, in both Hillington and Kinning Park, south of the Clyde. Similar difficulties have been experienced at Partick and to the west of the city centre. The significance of these materials, from the engineering point of view, is that driven piling is often permitted where there are few buildings nearby but is seldom permitted near existing tenemental properties or in gap sites. The approach works to the Clyde Tunnel southern access were constructed in materials of this nature and the vibrations associated with the works caused considerable distress to people living in the tenements at Linthouse. It is now a prerequisite to obtaining a building warrant that dilapidation surveys of nearby structures are carried out. If driven piling methods or ground improvement techniques involving vibrations are proposed, then monitoring must commence prior to the start of site works.

Many important developments in foundation construction occurred which quickly became accepted practice. These include:

- the use of a variety of piling methods;
- the use of different ground improvement techniques;
- advancement in the understanding and the prediction of settlement below buildings;
- understanding of resistance to uplift forces;
- advancements in methods of groundwater control, methods of land improvement and renewal (or restoration to a condition fit for future use) and
- the understanding of soil founding horizons and the interaction with the structure supported.

This list reads like a syllabus to a foundation engineering course but in concert with geology and geomorphology, all are interrelated. These factors, plus ground conditions and soil-structure interaction all form part of foundation engineering.

In the 1950s a Glasgow based construction company (Whatlings) introduced mechanical large-diameter-bore piling equipment from America which revolutionised the sinking of piles in Scotland. This equipment was to provide the piled foundations for many projects ranging from large buildings in the city centre to the foundations of the Ravenscraig steel works at Motherwell and Killroot Power Station in Northern Ireland.

The earlier piles were sunk using percussive methods still used today. The traditional techniques developed and evolved to provide pile installation suitable for a variety of soil and groundwater conditions. The larger diameter piles are now usually constructed using equipment known as the continuous flight auger which enables the material displaced to be replaced by concrete and a reinforcement cage to be added. Early research into the way in which the large diameter piles worked contributed to the overall understanding of piled foundations and future developments. Ironically some of the recent major buildings in the city centre were supported on a greater number of smaller piles.

It has long been recognised that all piling systems will cause disturbance but some systems minimise such effects. These systems are essential for new building in gap sites in the city centre. In a very few instances significant damage has occurred to adjacent properties and in the majority of these cases the piling triggered the event. It is probably realised by few people that even in difficult sites a piled foundation enables re-development with minimal disturbance in the immediate vicinity.

Many commercial structures and houses have been built on ground strengthened by the introduction of stone columns into the soil.

It is perhaps ironic that the dereliction of the dockland created areas that were infilled and then treated. The first inland dock created, Kingston Dock, was infilled and housing was erected, built on piled foundations. Both the larger Queens Docks and Prince's Docks were also infilled. In order to reduce the effect of settlements occurring between foundations placed on the existing quay wall and the infilling, the filled areas were compacted using dynamic compaction or consolidation techniques (the name depending on the proprietary system used). In this process a large weight, usually 8 to 20 tons, is dropped through a height, typically between 10 and 15 metres, in a grid pattern and the process repeated until a predetermined point is reached. Large-scale tests are then carried out to verify that the required degree of compaction has been achieved and that future settlements under any development proposed will be within closely defined parameters. In open spaces this method has been very successful but care is required when working in the vicinity of existing buildings. The Scottish Exhibition Conference Centre, a major hotel and most recently the 'Armadillo' building were built at the site of the former Queens Dock and the infilled Prince's Dock forms part of an area which will support housing, industrial development and a science park. Piled foundations were used to support the prominent v-shaped blocks of flats which border the river along the southern quays.

The land reclamation and improvement projects have also enabled areas that supported the giant Victorian works to be redeveloped. The former St Rollox works is now a major mail sorting office and distribution outlet. The very successful Cambuslang Investment Park is located on the platform which

previously supported a steel works and numerous railway sidings. In some instances these new buildings were located on piled foundations or on ground improved by vibro and dynamic compaction techniques.

It is perhaps ironic that dredging of the river has ceased, that quays remain quiet, and that early areas of the Industrial Revolution are forming the foundation to Glasgow's regeneration into the new millennium.

The recent history of Glasgow reflects the engineering achievements of the people, the strength and quality of the educational establishments and the foresight and acumen of the City Fathers. The Clyde was famous for the marine engineers who had 'served their time' and then travelled with their ships, taking with them their skills, ingenuity and expertise. The achievements of the engineers are often taken for granted, perhaps none more so than the work carried out by the foundation engineers and geotechnical specialists (soil mechanics and foundation engineering, mining engineering and geology). Their work is often buried and forgotten while structures above ground may remain to be admired for many generations.

As Glasgow declines from its great industrial past, the importance of the centre of learning continues. Founded in the 15th century and still flourishing today, education built upon a sound foundation has endured and continues to form the basis for the future.

The various engineering disciplines are fundamental to our modern society. Foundation or geotechnical engineering is one component, albeit perhaps the least recognised. Despite the tremendous changes that Glasgow has undergone, the process of learning from experience continues and enables the city to flourish and develop well into the future.

ACKNOWLEDGEMENTS
The author would like to thank Christina McAllister, May Allen, James Sutherland, Geoff Foord, David Martin, John Grant and the staff of the Glasgow City Archives for their assistance.

FIGURE 6
The River Clyde downstream of the Kingston Bridge, looking towards the Forum Hotel, and Armadillo.

The Luma Tower

The Luma Tower, originally built in 1938 as a light bulb factory and spectacularly remodelled as housing units 50 years later by Cornelius McClymont, is a striking example of Glasgow's regeneration in recent times. The listed Art Deco structure is one of Glasgow's landmarks, not just for travellers on the M8 but also for pilots landing at nearby Glasgow Airport.

Glasgow Development Agency, Atrium Court, 50 Waterloo Street, Glasgow, G2 6HQ

Glasgow Underground

(or, The Subway)

JIM SHIPWAY

INTRODUCTION

This account of Glasgow's Subway describes the influence of engineers not so much on building above the ground as below the ground, and their influence on one aspect of the life of our city – transport.

Just over 100 years ago, on 14 December 1896, Glasgow became the third city in the world after London and Budapest to declare open an underground passenger railway system. It had been under construction for more than five years and such was the crush and excitement on its opening day that several passengers were injured. The line had to close temporarily for five weeks and did not reopen until 21 January 1897. Though its engineering aspects and history are little known, the project contained many interesting features and most of these survive today (Figure 1).

The moving spirit behind the origin of the subway was a Lanarkshire civil and mining engineer, Alexander Simpson (1832-1922), who later became chairman of the Glasgow District Subway Co., the private company which

FIGURE 1
Early advertising poster of 1896.

FIGURE 2
The engineer and moving spirit of the Subway, Alexander Simpson (1832-1922).

FIGURE 3
Copland Road station as it was in 1897, showing cable traction. The modernised station (1978) is now re-named Ibrox.

built and operated the Subway in its early days (Figure 2). In 1923 it was taken over by the then Glasgow Corporation, and in 1935 the system was electrified. In this year there was also an official change of name, and the Subway became the 'Underground'. Whether this was an instance of the City Fathers deliberating aping London is hard to say, but Glaswegians still refer affectionately to the 'Subway'. The name has stuck, and will be used throughout this chapter. After all, many cities of the world have an Underground, but what other city has a Subway?

The most interesting feature of the Subway's early days was its method of traction, which was by an endless cable running on sheaves between the rails. It was not the first cable-operated underground railway in Britain, for cable haulage had been used briefly in 1870 for a crossing under the Thames, and was also widely used for street tramways and in mines. In Glasgow, the Subway continued to use cable haulage for nearly 40 years until electrification in 1935, (Figure 3).

The scale of the work involved in the building of the Subway was immense. Its construction in 1890-96 took place almost concurrently with the rebuilding of the Tay Bridge (1882-87) and the building of the Forth Bridge (1883-90). As a comparison, the new Tay Bridge cost £670,000 and took five years to build, the Subway cost £1.59 million and took 5½ years to build, and the Forth Bridge cost £2.60 million and was 7 years in building. The construction of the Subway was therefore one of the major public works of the time in Britain. Further, it was financed, not by a prosperous group of giant railway companies, but by a small group of Scots industrialists who formed the Glasgow District Subway Company. Their farsightedness reaches even to our lives today in travelling in Glasgow, and has done so for over 100 years.

THE SUBWAY'S ORIGINS

The expansion of the city during the latter half of the 19th century was rapid and by the 1880s it had become the second city of the British Empire. It had also become seriously congested. Horses and carts, vans, omnibuses and cabs jostled for road space with the horse-drawn trams. This situation was not unique to Glasgow and in London a similar problem had been alleviated by going underground. Glasgow already had, or planned, two long stretches of main line railway running in tunnels under the city from east to west. The Glasgow City & District Railway was opened in 1886 at which time the Glasgow Central Railway was under construction. These lines set a precedent and encouraged the idea of further underground extensions to link the developing shopping and residential western area of the city with its commercial centre. Strangely, the eastern area of Glasgow with its works and factories and teeming populace did not appear in the original proposals, though extensions may have been envisaged for this at some time in the future.

Thus the Glasgow District Subway Company was formed in 1887 and promoted a bill in that year for Parliamentary powers to construct an underground railway. The proposal was for a line 2.75 miles in length running roughly east-west in a semi-circle north of the Clyde between Buchanan Street and Partick. It was to have six stations less than half a mile apart and a single tunnel 3.66 m in diameter. The bill was rejected by the Commons, seemingly because it was unsuitable for its purpose.

In the following year a second scheme was promoted. This was more than twice the size of the first, being 6.5 miles in length and having twin tunnels. It passed under the Clyde at two points in a roughly circular shape in plan, linking areas both north and south of the river. Its estimated cost was £677,000. This scheme was opposed by the Clyde Trustees among others who contended that the proposed level of the subway tunnels under the Clyde would restrict dredging and deepening of the river. Chiefly for this reason Parliament rejected this second scheme.

However in 1889 the Glasgow Harbour Tunnel Company had obtained approval for the construction of a group of three tunnels at Finnieston for vehicles and pedestrians. This opened the door to under-river tunnelling for the Subway company, who submitted a third proposal in 1890.

The third scheme (Figure 4) differed little from the second, but offered greater clearance for the under-river sections, and was not opposed by the Clyde Trustees. It was passed by Parliament in 1890. This was for an underground railway 6.55 miles long in double tunnels, wholly underground, to be worked by any means other than steam locomotives. The gauge was to be the standard 4ft 8½in (1.43 m) but a later Act of 1894 altered this to 'not less than 3'6"' (1.07 m). The gauge actually adopted was 4.0 ft (1.22 m), which meant that in the future there was to be no possibility of interchange of rolling stock with other existing railways.

The total cost eventually amounted to £1.59 million, some of this arising from the course of the Subway tunnels under private property in the city. The company was forced to buy all the property under which the line passed to obtain wayleave and avoid disputes. At the same time the choice of route was chosen as far as possible to lie under streets, which offered free wayleave. In the

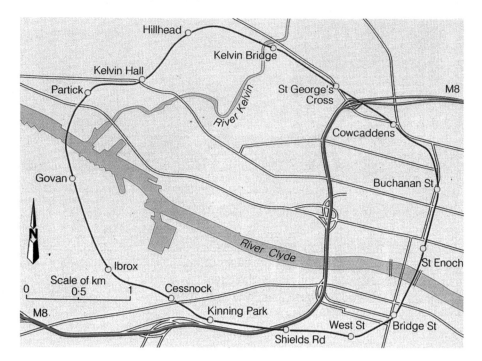

FIGURE 4
Plan of the 6.55
mile Subway route
and its 15 stations.

section between Govan and Kinning Park the ground was largely undeveloped, and the line was constructed partly under open fields.

Earlier tunnelling ventures in Glasgow had revealed that the geology of Glasgow was far from attractive for underground railway construction, and likely to lead to greater expense than, say, ground conditions in London. The Clyde was also another obstacle. In 1890 no tunnel existed under Glasgow's river, though in England both the Mersey and Severn tunnels had been completed in 1886 and there were other tunnel river crossings in London of which the first was Brunel's Thames tunnel completed nearly 50 years before in 1843.

OTHER CONTEMPORARY UNDERGROUND RAILWAYS

London had an Underground as far as back as 1863, when the first section of the Metropolitan line was opened. The Inner Circle, completed in 1884, was mainly constructed by cut-and-cover methods (see later) rather than tunnelling, and was worked by steam locomotives whose smoke and fumes were a source of some irritation to passengers. The City & South London Railway was built in 1886-90 and was first planned as a cable railway but was eventually worked by electric locomotives. It ran between Stockwell and the City, a distance of some 3 miles, wholly in twin tunnels.

Abroad, the first city in Europe to have an Underground was Budapest whose line opened in May 1896, seven months ahead of Glasgow. This railway was again operated by steam locomotives and built mainly by cut-and-cover.

Proposals for an Underground in Paris were authorised in 1898 and the first section opened in 1900; the whole scheme was not completed until several years later. New York's Underground was opened in 1905 some years after the early advances in Europe.

It will be seen from the above that the Glasgow Subway made a remarkably early appearance on the 'underground stage'. The variety of difficult geological conditions inevitably delayed its completion and allowed Budapest to become the second Underground to open after London's.

THE ENGINEERS

Large and prestigious public works constructed in Scotland in the 19th century often attracted firms from London or the south (as happens today.) For example, Glasgow's water supply from Loch Katrine in the 1850s was engineered by J.F.T. Bateman; the Tay bridges of 1878 and 1887 were designed by Sir Thomas Bouch and William Barlow respectively; the Forth Bridge of 1883-90 was designed by Sir John Fowler and Sir Benjamin Baker; and much of the massive Caledonian Railway work was engineered by Sir John Wolfe Barry.

The promoters of the Subway however chose a local Glasgow firm of modest size, Simpson & Wilson. This may have been because the senior partner, Alexander Simpson (1832-1922) had a long connection with the mining industry in Lanarkshire, or more likely, the firm had a record of tunnel construction for the City & District Railway (1886), the planning of the Harbour Tunnel (1890-5) and in railway construction both in Scotland and abroad. The firm was later to be appointed engineers for the Mallaig extension of the West Highland Railway (1897-1901) and for the delicate underpinning and restoration of the Auld Brig of Ayr, a 15th century medieval bridge, in 1907.

The greater part of the Subway's engineering was carried out by Alexander Simpson's son and partner Robert (1859-1931), an enthusiastic bachelor who practically lived on the job for five years. However the father was enthusiastic too, as it is on record that he returned by ship to Glasgow from a visit to railway works in the West Indies, and instead of heading for home, went straight to visit the Subway construction!

The mechanical and electrical engineering work of the Subway, which was considerable, was undertaken by David Hume Morton, whose firm was later to be associated with major improvements to the main drainage of Glasgow in 1904.

METHOD OF TRACTION AND ITS INFLUENCE

For economy's sake the tunnels were made as small as possible commensurate with rolling stock which would accommodate standing passengers without excessive discomfort. This led to a tunnel diameter of 3.35 m and a rail gauge of 1.22 m. This tunnel diameter compares with the 3.81 m in tunnels of London's Victoria Line today (see Figure 5).

This choice of gauge was somewhat unusual as all other main line railways in Britain had a gauge of 4 ft 8½in (1.43 m). However, the Glasgow Subway was entirely enclosed, a continuous circuit with no connection to any other railway. With the tunnel diameter fixed at 3.35 m, there was no way standard railway rolling stock could have been accommodated. It was therefore entirely logical to fix the gauge to suit the Subway. This choice has been vindicated, for over the 100 years of its life no operational disadvantage has been experienced.

The method of traction chosen was by an endless cable mounted between the rails. The layout of the Subway involved very steep gradients of 1 in 20 at

FIGURE 5
Cast-iron ringed
tunnel, ballasted
track and cable on
sheaves.

the river crossings and a short length of 1 in 18 elsewhere. These gradients led to reservations about the necessary adhesion between wheels and rails being adequate if the trains were self-propelled. In addition, the motors available for electric traction at the time were heavy and bulky, and could not be accommodated easily under the car floors. Separate locomotives, or battery locomotives, would occupy valuable platform space at stations, lead to extra wear and tear on the rails, and require a heavier rail and further, the engineering of electric traction was in its infancy and something of an unknown quantity.

Cable haulage, on the other hand, was well understood, and was adopted only after an exhaustive survey of systems of traction both in the UK and the USA. It had the advantages of being clean and free from fumes. The endless cable to which the trains attached themselves revolved at a constant speed of about 21.7 km/h, and trains going downhill assisted those going uphill. It allowed maximum space for passengers in the cars, owing to the absence of mechanical plant. The main disadvantage was that considerable skill was required by the train driver (the 'gripman') in picking up and releasing the cable, and achieving smooth starting and stopping of the trains (Figure 3).

The vertical curve of the cable was limited to 762 m radius at the steepest gradients in order that the cable under tension would not lift off the sheaves, and even bear against the tunnel roof. Careful calculations were made, but it was rumoured that no one was really sure until opening day, with fully-loaded trains, whether the cable would behave as predicted. Fortunately it did.

The adoption of cable haulage and the acceptance of steep gradients allowed the adoption of 'humps' at stations. This idea had first been put forward by Sir John Fowler, the engineer of the Metropolitan and Inner Circle lines in London, in his address to the British Association in 1882, when he said:

Comparatively high speed and economy of working might be attained on a railway with stations at half mile intervals, if it were possible to arrange the gradients so that each station should be on the summit of a hill. An ideal railway would have gradients of about 1 in 20 falling away from the stations, with a piece of level horizontal track connecting them ...

The value of this observation was evidently not lost on the engineers of the Subway. The 15 stations are an average of 0.44 miles (0.71 km) apart, and braking and acceleration is assisted at several by gradients of 1 in 20 on each side. The close spacing of the stations, however, left little room for the horizontal stretch between gradients.

This spacing of the stations is, with the exception of Paris, the closest of any urban underground railway system in the world. The average of 0.44 miles compares with 1.13 miles on London's Metropolitan Line, and exercises a decisive influence on scheduled speed. For this reason, the Subway will never be one of the fastest underground rail systems, but the siting of the stations was obviously (and rightly) for the convenience of passengers. The endless cables (one for each tunnel) weighed 57 tons each and were powered by steam engines. Electricity for lighting and signalling was generated in a power house also requiring steam engines. The engines and mechanical plant were housed in buildings built for the purpose in Scotland Street which still exist. These mechanical and electrical aspects of the Subway required considerable engineering input, but space does not allow a description here.

The wholly underground nature of the Subway, with no rail connection to the surface, led to the requirement of a special pit and overhead crane for servicing of the cars. They were lifted bodily off the track and deposited in the car shed. This unusual arrangement, though somewhat cumbersome, worked well for 80 years before modernisation (Figure 6).

FIGURE 6
Subway car lifted off track through pit for servicing.

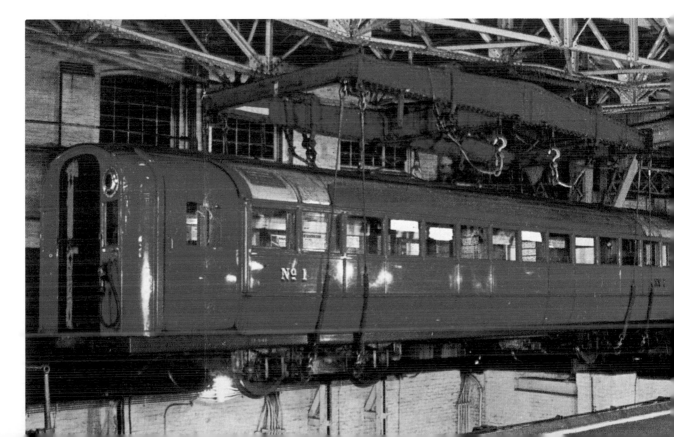

THE GEOLOGY OF THE SUBWAY'S ROUTE

Beginning at Buchanan Street Station, if the route is followed clockwise the sequence of material encountered was approximately as follows:

1. Buchanan Street to Bridge Street, with river crossing (1226 m) – sand and silt
2. Bridge Street to Shields Road (1120 m) – firm to stiff clay.
3. Shields Road to Govan (2888 m) – sand, silty sand and occasional clay.
4. Govan to Partick (853 m) – sand and silt, with some boulder clay and rock at the river crossing.
5. Partick to Buchanan Street (4,453 m) – sedimentary rocks, shale, occasional old coal workings and a flooded quarry.

It will be seen that north of the Clyde, where the ground level was higher, the geology of the route was mainly sedimentary rocks and shale, i.e. about 2.77 miles or 42% of the Subway's total length.

The remaining 58% (3.78 miles) consisted mainly of alluvial material – clays, sands and silt, much of it water bearing and lying almost entirely to the south of the Clyde excepting the length between Buchanan Street and St Enoch stations.

It was this soft material which formed the most difficult part of the construction, particularly the river crossings. Tunnelling in rock was relatively straightforward apart from influxes of water. A buried quarry near Glasgow Street in Hillhead contributed its share and flooded the tunnels when encountered. There are many hidden filled-in quarries in the north and west of Glasgow and it was perhaps fortunate that the route of the Subway met only one of them.

Construction began at St Enoch Station in March 1891, involving a deep excavation in water-bearing sand.

TUNNELLING METHODS IN ALLUVIAL MATERIALS

The depth from ground level to the tunnels' formation level* was significant in the choice of method. Shallow construction, where the depth was not greater than 9.14 m allowed cut-and-cover to be used in places rather than tunnelling. Altogether three methods designed to suit the various soft ground conditions were employed as follows:

(a) **Cut and cover** (Figures 7 and 8)

Two rows of timber sheet piling 8.38 m (27½ft) apart were driven to formation level, and the ground between excavated to the level of the underside of the tunnels' double concrete arch (the upper concrete in Figure 7). The bottom of this excavation was shaped to the profile of the arches' undersides, and spaces cut in the piling at intervals to provide a bearing for the arch haunches, which were then cast. The top of the arches was covered with two coats of asphalt for waterproofing. The excavation was then filled in and the ground surface, whether roadway or unoccupied, restored.

---

*formation level – the surface level after the digging but before concreting.

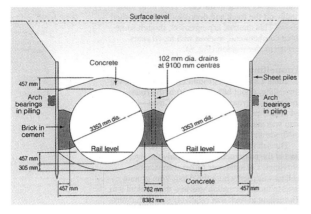

FIGURE 7
Cross-section of cut-and-cover tunnel construction
(from original drawing).

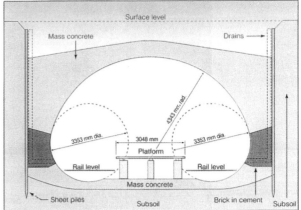

FIGURE 8
Station construction in cut-and-cover
(from original drawing).

The ground between the piles under the concrete arches was then excavated, one tunnel at a time. One half of the double invert was laid, and one side wall and one side of the centre wall built in brickwork. After a 4.57 m (15 ft) length had been completed the second tunnel was built in a similar manner.

When passing through vacant ground this method was varied according to the contractor's choice. Sometimes the excavation was carried down to formation level, the piles being strutted apart, and the arches of the tunnel roof constructed with centring.

Where the ground was water-bearing sand, the material at first entered the excavation through joints in the sheet piling. When this happened, settlement of the buildings at street level began to occur, as might be expected. However, it was discovered, almost by chance, that if the piling was tight and only water entered the excavation, without carrying sand with it, then no settlement took place. Thus it was learned that dry sand and fully saturated sand have the same volume. Thereafter, great care was taken in built-up areas to allow no sand to escape into open excavations, water only being pumped out.

In some places the material was water-bearing and soft such that at the level of the invert (the concrete at the base of the tunnel) the ground could not bear the weight of the concrete. Air-pressure was then employed to force back the water and dry out the formation. There was often a large escape of air at the sides of the arch, but a pressure of 14 kN/sq m to 21 kN/sq m was sufficient and achieved without difficulty, allowing the invert to be constructed.

The average speed achieved by the cut-and-cover method was 42.67 m (140 ft) per month of finished work, the maximum speed being 85.34 m (280 ft) in one month. This required the opening up of a considerable length of construction at any one time, but under the streets this length was limited, as the Subway Act of 1890 prohibited the opening up of more than 30.48 m (100 ft) at a time, and the openings had to be at least 137.2 m apart. The speed of construction under the streets as a result slowed to an average of 27.43 m (90 ft) per month, the greatest length in any one month being 38.71 m (127 ft).

(b) Tunnelling at depth in alluvial material

Where the tunnels were in water-bearing strata at a depth greater than 9.14 m (30 ft), or the ground surface could not be opened up (as at the Clyde crossings), the construction required a watertight lining of iron rings, built in segments, and the use of a shield under compressed air (Figure 9).

The iron tunnel lining comprised rings each 3.66 m (12 ft) external diameter and 0.46 m (1½ ft) in width. Each ring was made up of nine equal segments with a smaller closing segment at the crown. The joint between each segment was formed of softwood between bolted faces, (Figure 10), a detail which led to much discussion between tunnelling engineers of the day, but which proved watertight and was easily constructed.

The shield (Figure 9) was a cylindrical shell 3.72 m (12¼ ft) in external diameter and 1.98 m (6½ ft) in overall length, built up from 6.4 mm (¼") thick steel plates. One end of the shell was fitted with the cutting edge, and about 0.30 m (1 ft) back from this was the bulkhead of 19 mm (¾") steel plate with a sliding door to give access to the face. The shield was controlled by six hydraulic rams located round the circumference. Any one of the rams could be worked independently of the others, allowing the direction of travel to be altered as required. Each shield with its fittings weighed six tons. The rams pressed against the rings of the completed tunnel, forcing the shield forward as the work advanced, and the iron rings were built up inside the shield and were grouted as the shield moved forward.

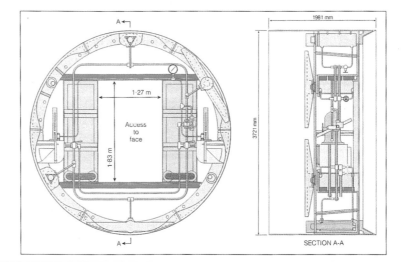

FIGURE 9
Shield used in tunnel construction in water-bearing soft ground (from original drawing).

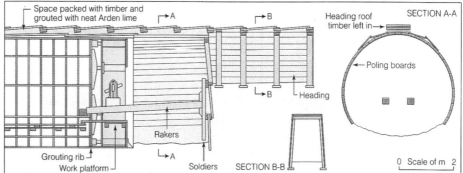

FIGURE 10
Support arrangement for excavation ahead of shield (from original drawing).

The ground ahead of the shield was excavated for a length of about 2.74 m (9 ft) using poling boards closely fitted round the circumference of the tunnel, (Figure 10) and grouted. The shield was then moved into this space. It was found that using this method under compressed air, the shield was of very little advantage, and some of the contractors abandoned its use. Working in sand required the use of poling boards, and the compressed air stiffened the ground, rendering the shield to some extent superfluous.

Difficulties were experienced however at the river crossing at Custom House Quay. Here the cover to the top of the tunnel was a mere 4.27 m (14 ft) of sand and silt, increasing to 8.84 m (29 ft) across the width of the river. Before the first, westernmost tunnel had advanced 24.4 m (80 ft) under the river, the bed had 'blown up' no less than ten times. The worst burst created a hole 7.31 m (24 ft) square and 4.88 m (16 ft) deep, fortunately without loss of life. The contractor asked to be relieved of the work, and a second contractor, George Talbot, was appointed. He carefully regulated the air pressure according to the state of the tide, and successfully completed both tunnels. This distance of 125 m (410 ft) for the second, easternmost, tunnel was completed in 14 weeks, including time spent in restoring the working after one blowout.

(c) Tunnelling in clay (Figure 11)

The clay encountered was impervious to water and occurred mainly at places where some settlement of the surface ground could be tolerated. In this situation, ordinary brick tunnel lining was used, being cheaper than iron rings, though slower to construct and therefore offering a greater possibility of settlement at the surface.

The brick tunnels are circular both internally and externally. The lowest quadrant was constructed in mass concrete, and the remainder in four rings of brick in cement. The construction was done in 2.74 m (9 ft) lengths, and the rate of progress was about 22.3 m (73 ft) per month, the maximum rate in one month being 28.3 m (93 ft).

In one area of clay, where the Subway passed under the Caledonian Railway running east-west, it was absolutely necessary to avoid settlement, and here an iron lining was used in conjunction with a shield, but without the use of compressed air. This was the only part of the Subway where this method was used. The advantage of the shield here was that the bore of the shield allowed the closest approximation to the diameter of the finished tunnel, and the risk of settlement was kept to a minimum. The annular space of 6 cm between shield and iron rings was grouted.

(d) Tunnelling in rock (Figure 12)

A long stretch of the Subway on the north side of the Clyde, about 2.77 miles, is in rock, chiefly sandstone and shale. Here the work was laborious rather than difficult. The material was removed by explosives, the tunnel interior trimmed and then lined with two to four rings of brick in cement, or concrete.

One of the contractors in particular, Robert McAlpine & Co., chose to use mass concrete rather than brickwork and the thickness of this varied from 229 mm to 457 mm (9 to 18 inches). This form of lining was unusual at that

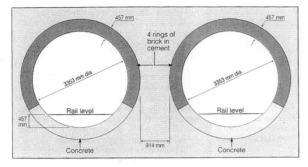

FIGURE 11
Tunnel lining in clay – rings of brick-in-cement.

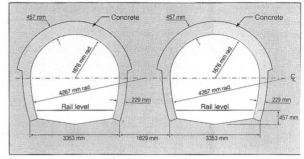

FIGURE 12
Tunnel lining in rock by Robert McAlpine, using concrete.

time. In places the rock was of sufficiently good quality to be used as aggregate for the concrete. The mix used was 'five parts of broken rock to one part of cement, with sand as required'.

A seam of old coal wastes (voids) which underlies part of the Hillhead area was encountered. Here the voids had to have substantial structures of brickwork built within them to resist the thrust of the arched roofs of the tunnels. This seam of coal outcropped on the banks of the Kelvin, and when the river was high it flooded the coal wastes and greatly impeded the work.

When the tunnels lay under main streets, shafts were sunk in side streets, usually about a quarter-mile apart, and drifts (i.e. short tunnels) constructed to the line of the main tunnels.

The River Kelvin was crossed by first building a cofferdam across half its width and excavating a trench in the rock of the river bed of sufficient depth and width to allow rings of iron lining to be laid in place. The cover to the river bed was approximately 0.6 m, and this was filled with concrete. The other half of the distance, a little over 15 m was constructed in the same way.

STATIONS

According to the depths of the tunnels, stations were constructed either in tunnel, by cut-and-cover, or in the open between retaining walls. The shallowest station, Kinning Park was only 4.27 m (14 ft) from ground to platform level and was constructed by the latter method. The deepest station, 12.2 m (40 ft), is Buchanan Street.

As originally constructed the fifteen stations were of the island platform type, approximately 46 m (151 ft) long x 8.5 m (28 ft) wide, the platform being 3.0 m wide. Generally the two rail tunnels merge into one arch forming the roof of the station, which was from 3.35 m to 4.9 m (11 to 16 ft) above the platform at its crown. The platforms and stairs were largely of timber construction, as were parts of the roof. This possible fire hazard caused unease among some of the citizens. Fortunately it proved unfounded.

Eight of the 15 stations were wholly or partially-lit by glass roofs (Figure 3). Others depended on seven or eight pairs of 16 candle-power lamps. Today this would be considered totally inadequate and even at the turn of the century it was obviously poor. Whitewashing the walls did not help much, and the stations often appeared dingy and dull.

In built up areas, entrances to stations were often through shop premises converted for the purpose. Others had plain architect-designed small buildings in brick. The showpiece station of the Subway was St Enoch (Figure 13) which was designed by James Miller, the leading railway architect of the time. He was also the architect, in 1913, of the Institution of Civil Engineers headquarters in Great George Street, Westminster, London.

The major overhaul of the Subway in 1977-80 involved the reconstruction of some of the stations and a general upgrading of the others (Figure 14).

CONTRACTORS

There were eight main contractors involved in the civil engineering work of the Subway between 1891-96. Most were well-known and highly experienced public works contractors of the day, as follows (construction lengths in brackets):

George Talbot – (1228 m)
David Shanks – (453 m)
Charles Brand & Son – (1938 m)
John Paterson & Sons Ltd – (1122 m)
Hugh Kennedy & Sons – (2340 m)
Watt & Wilson – (1209 m)
James Smith & Co – (747 m)
Robert McAlpine & Co – (1504 m)

The only surviving contractor of the list appears to be Robert McAlpine & Company (now Sir Robert McAlpine & Sons Ltd.). They completed the section between Buchanan Street and Cowcaddens Stations, mostly in rock. This section, which was McAlpine's first tunnelling contract, was completed by April 1894 after two years' work. The approximate contract value was £65,000. The tunnels were lined with concrete, and the engineers commented:

> '... Almost all the rock tunnels have been lined, and this has been done with concrete – a method initiated by Mr Robert McAlpine, and which, when well done, makes an admirable lining.'

Of the remaining contractors, Hugh Kennedy & Sons were simultaneously engaged on the construction of the Harbour Tunnel, (1889-95) and George Talbot also completed the Mound Tunnel in Edinburgh at about the same time. This latter firm successfully completed the Clyde river crossings for the Subway when the contractors who originally tendered got into difficulties. Charles Brand & Son were perhaps the best known of the list after McAlpine, and continued trading until recent years. Between them these four contractors – Talbot, Brand, Kennedy and McAlpine – completed two-thirds of the Subway's total length.

ELECTRIFICATION

In 1923 the Subway was purchased and taken over by Glasgow Corporation, and it became one undertaking with the Tramways Department. In 1928 the undertaking became known as the Glasgow Corporation Transport Department.

FIGURE 13
Painting of St. Enoch station building by A. P. Thomson R.S.W. (c. 1900).

FIGURE 14
Govan Station under reconstruction in 1977. Cast iron tunnel rings are seen on the right.

Plans for electrification had been considered before the 1914-18 war, and were raised again in 1922, but it was 1933 before tests were completed sufficiently for a final decision to be taken. Conversion was finally completed by December 1935. The existing rolling stock was converted from cable to electric traction, and the existing 30 kg/m rails were relaid with 40 kg/m flat-bottomed rails. The 30 kg/m rails were reused as conductor rails for the power supply. The track remained ballasted, with tile drains.

The electrical system employed was 600 volts DC, and the complete electrification cost £94,000 against the considerable annual outlay of £10,000 in maintaining cable operation. Under cable traction the maximum speed of the trains had been about 22.5 km/h. Electrification enabled this speed to be increased to 29 km/h.

The Corporation at this time attempted to create a new image for the Subway and they renamed it the Underground. After electrification, the Subway became more popular and numbers using it increased, rising to a maximum of 37 million/year in 1949-50.

MODERNISATION 1977-80

By the 1960s the Subway had become archaic and worn-out. Frequent breakdowns were commonplace and despite valiant work by the maintenance staff it was becoming obvious that it was nearing the end of its useful life. Plans for modernisation were prepared and the Subway finally closed in May 1977 for a comprehensive programme to begin.

During the time 1896-1977, a period of 81 years, the original rolling stock had continued in use. The passenger cars had been designed by the original mechanical and electrical engineer to the company, D.H. Morton, and built by the Oldbury Railway Carriage & Wagon Company of Birmingham. Their amazing durability had rendered the Subway almost a piece of industrial archaeology in its own lifetime.

Civil engineering aspects of the modernisation programme included:

(a) The removal of the old ballasted trackwork and its replacement with new track laid on a concrete base.
(b) The construction of access railtracks from the tunnels to the car sheds, eliminating the lifting pit for servicing the cars.
(c) Fire exits at each station and escalators where appropriate.
(d) The construction of a new interchange station at Partick (formally Merkland Street) and an increase in the size and number of platforms of certain stations to accommodate longer trains and ease passenger movement.
(e) Several new station buildings and entrances.
(f) New workshop building, yard and test tracks.

There was also a major mechanical and electrical engineering input, together with signalling and control systems and new rolling stock. The total cost amounted to £60 million. The journey time was decreased from 28 minutes to 22 minutes for a circuit of the 6.55 mile system. Present usage of the Subway is about 14.8 million passengers per year.

The consulting engineers for the civil engineering works were Sir William Halcrow & Partners together with Merz & McLellan for the electrical and mechanical works.

The modernisation has transformed the Subway from the former somewhat cramped and dingy appearance of the stations and buildings to well-lit pleasing and attractive buildings with excellent amenities for passengers and staff. The rolling stock has undergone a similar transformation, and new life has been breathed into the whole system. It seems that the Subway is set to roll on its way for a second hundred years of existence, maintaining its unique service to the city of Glasgow.

ACKNOWLEDGEMENTS
The author would like to acknowledge assistance given by Mary Murphy, archivist of the Institution of Civil Engineers in tracing and supplying information, and John Wright of Strathclyde Passenger Transport Executive likewise for information and assistance. Sir William Halcrow & Partners, Glasgow were also helpful in this regard.

REFERENCES
Anonymous *Glasgow District Subway: Its Construction and Equipment*. 1905.

Burdon, I.P., Middleton, A.G. The reconstruction of the Glasgow Underground Railway. *Electronics & Power*. May 1982, p.396.

Coombs, D.H., Willson, G.J. The trend of development in the Design and Equipment of Underground Railways. *Proceedings of the Institution of Civil Engineers*, October 1953, p. 605.

Mackay, Thomas. *Life of Sir John Fowler*. John Murray, London, 1900, p. 164.

Morton, A.H. *The Glasgow District Subway*. Maclure, Macdonald & Co., Glasgow, 1897.

Russell, I.F. *Sir Robert McAlpine & Sons* – The Early Years. (Private publication).

Shipway, J.S., The Centenary of the Glasgow Subway, 1896-1996. *Proceedings of the Institution of Civil Engineers*, August 1996, p.130.

Simpson, Robert. Construction of the Glasgow City & District Railway. *Transactions Institution of Engineers and Shipbuilders in Scotland*. **xxxi**, 1887-88, p. 13.

Simpson, Robert. Tunnelling in soft material with reference to Glasgow District Subway. *Transactions Institution of Engineers & Shipbuilders in Scotland*. **xxxix**, 1895-96, p. 129.

Stewart, A.M. (student's paper) The Glasgow District Subway. *Minutes of Proceedings, Institution of Civil Engineers*, **122**, 1895, p.355.

Thomson, D.L., Sinclair, D.E. *The Glasgow Subway*. Scottish Tramway Museum Society, Glasgow, 1964.

PHOTOGRAPHS & DIAGRAMS
Figures 4,7,8,9,10,11 and 12 are from *Proceedings of the Institution of Civil Engineers*, Civil Engineering, August 1996, Vol. 114 Issue 3 by courtesy of Thomas Telford Publishing.

*End note: Many measurements are given in both imperial and metric forms.
For dimensions without a conversion the following factors can be applied:
to convert metres to feet, multiply by 3.28: feet to metres, 0.3; miles to kilometres, 1.6: kilometres to miles, 0.625.

Holmwood House

Described as Alexander 'Greek' Thomson's finest villa, Holmwood House in Cathcart was officially opened to the public on 29 August 1998 by the National Trust for Scotland. Babtie Group acted as Consulting Engineer on the restoration of this superb Neo-Classical example of Thomson's architecture and interior design.

Babtie Group, 95 Bothwell Street, Glasgow, G2 7HX

Lion Chambers

ARTHUR BRYAN

At the time of publication, this unique A-listed building selected by Historic Scotland as a building of historical interest will lie shrouded in scaffolding tubes and protective netting, hidden from public view.

The eight-storey structure standing 90 feet above pavement level is now unoccupied with the exception of the ground floor and basement. It was designed and built in 1904-1907 and is now suffering the wear and tear of being exposed to the west of Scotland weather for nearly a century, the effects of which were probably never fully anticipated by the designers.

In 1904, Mr William George Black, a Glasgow lawyer, writer, and member of the Glasgow Art Club commissioned a firm of local architects, Salmon & Gillespie, to design a building to accommodate lawyers on the upper floors (first to seventh floor levels) and with an artist's studio on the top floor and a printers and stationers occupying the ground floor and basement.

The task facing the architect and the builder was considerable. The site chosen by William Black was situated on the east side of Hope Street in the centre of a bustling city, with an existing building occupying the ground to the south, a small cart lane to the north and a neighbour's boundary wall to the east. In fact, it was not much larger than two semi-detached houses. In view of its location in the city, further restrictions were imposed on the builder during the construction stage by the city authorities.

Due to the restricted size of the site, it was necessary for the architect to consider ways of gaining useable space. To achieve larger offices, he adopted a quite new and in many ways revolutionary technique which was certainly new to Britain at that time, called the Hennebique system. The design and construction being offered by Hennebique employed the use of reinforced concrete throughout with small internal columns and an external wall supporting the concrete floors. The external load-bearing walls were only four inches thick and thus provided the architect with the additional space he was looking for. Whilst the system had been in limited use in England since 1898, this was the first reinforced concrete building of its kind in Scotland.

It was in 1892 that François Hennebique, a French contractor, obtained a British patent for his specialized system and in 1897 appointed L.G. Mouchel as his agent for any work undertaken in Britain. Despite considerable competition from other specialist systems, his business grew at an astonishing

FIGURE 1
The location of the Lion Chambers in central Glasgow.

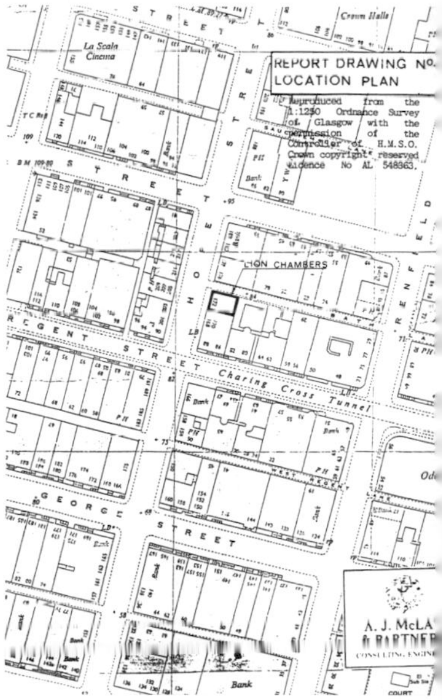

pace and by 1909 the Hennebique Company could boast 62 offices scattered throughout Europe, USA, Asia and Africa. It seems that there was a pent-up demand for someone to design and construct an economical structure which provided far greater fire resistance than the iron or steel structures which had dominated the 19th century.

The term reinforced concrete, used to describe the mixing of steel reinforcement and a concrete mix made up of sand, aggregate, and cement, has been adopted in more recent times. The system being developed by François Hennebique around the turn of the century was better known as 'ferro-concrete' or 'ferrocrete'.

This form of construction was growing rapidly throughout the world around this time but the adoption of the Hennebique technique for the Lion Chambers building was very innovative and could be described as a pioneering undertaking. It is not surprising that when construction started in 1905, the activities attracted great interest not only from local folk, but from local builders who gathered in Hope Street to watch this new phenomenon take shape. It should be remembered that due to its height the structure dwarfed the buildings to the north and south and significantly altered the landscape of the east side of Hope Street.

Around this time it was extremely rare for an independent consulting engineer to be involved in building design of this kind, and architects were considered technically competent to design the structure of relatively simple masonry buildings. Elements of the buildings such as floors, roofs, walls, and foundations were sized by using standard tables or rule of thumb methods and did not require calculations. However when it came to more demanding structures such as reinforced concrete or structural steelwork, particularly of extended height, then the services of a specialist were called for, hence the arrival of François Hennebique. His design was based on the use of mild steel reinforcement as plain round bars and these were held together with a mixture of flat steel or wire strips. As is common in modern-day construction, the strength of some elements of buildings are established by full scale tests and the design follows along behind. Such was the case for François Hennebique who applied his considerable technical skills and experience to the market opening up before him.

It is not clear how the architect and the specialist contractor worked together and to what extent the specialist imposed his system on the scheme developed by the architect. It seems likely that control of the structural layout was in the hands of the specialist, who was continually developing his system, project by project.

When compared with the modern-day construction methods and sophisticated plant available, it is difficult to comprehend the task facing the builder on this congested site in 1905. The small footprint of the building, occupying every square inch available, was not helped by the restrictions imposed on his operations. He was allowed to occupy three feet of the lane to the north, maintaining cart traffic at all times, and six feet of Hope Street to the west. He had insufficient space to erect an external scaffold to allow access to the upper floors and resorted to a flying scaffold which was supported off each floor and was moved up floor by floor. All materials were hoisted by

FIGURE 2
The Lion Chambers stands stark and proud against the backdrop of other Glasgow buildings.

hand, floor by floor, and of course placed in the shutters (part of the form-work which held the concrete in place until it set) by hand. Mechanical compaction was not introduced until the 1920s and so to ensure that the concrete surrounded the reinforcement and filled all corners of the shutters, a high slump or wetter concrete mix was adopted.

The lack of any working space on the site prevented the use of any power plant with the result that every bucket or barrow of concrete was mixed by hand, hoisted by hand and placed by hand.

In common with many buildings in the city centre, a basement was formed which occupied the entire plan area of the site, and despite the presence of an adjoining building to the south, and a main city thoroughfare to the west, any difficulties were taken in their stride and the work completed. It is no wonder that passers by stopped and watched in utter amazement at this Glasgow 'skyscraper' rising before them.

Reinforced concrete provided the architect with an opportunity to capitalize on the restrictions of the site, and to express the desired external appearance of the building with the actual structural form. The external concrete finish selected by the architect was either a plain surface or comprised ornamental or decorative motifs. The Lion Chambers building displays both to great effect. It is perhaps the combination of both structure and external design that gives the building its undisputed place in the history of Glasgow architecture.

There are two other aspects of reinforced concrete that should be mentioned, one of which was certainly understood by Hennebique, the other perhaps not. An inbuilt benefit of reinforced concrete was its natural ability to withstand fire thus obviating the need for any further protective coatings or finishes. Whilst there was a general understanding that the concrete cover protected the reinforcement from fire, it was extremely unlikely that the depths of concrete required to act as a protective barrier were known or fully understood. The failure however to understand the significance of the problems of durability of concrete exposed to the external elements has

FIGURE 3
One of the ornamental motifs, showing signs of age.

resulted in many buildings suffering serious structural distress. This comment is not intended to be a criticism of Hennebique as it is only in the last 20 years or so that we have begun to understand the effects of the acid environment on structures and the importance attached to acknowledging durability at the time of design and construction.

It is precisely this problem that has befallen the external wall and the lowest floor of the Lion Chambers and resulted in scaffolding protection being necessary around the building. There is in fact a touch of irony in the necessity in the 1990s to erect a protective scaffold, when in 1905 the builder was not able to erect a street scaffold due to restrictions placed upon him by the authorities.

FIGURE 4
The Lion Chambers completely enshrouded by scaffolding and netting, hopefully to emerge in refurbished state.

FIGURE 5
The gradual deterioration of the structure has revealed the mild steel reinforcement bars, the interconnecting strips and strips of wire.

The external wall is the cause of most concern. It is simply too thin – with two layers of reinforcement contained within four inches – and it was only a matter of time before the effects of the weather and contaminants in the environment began to take their toll. It is almost inconceivable that the structure has managed to survive 90 years when by modern codes of practice it should have long since disappeared.

In terms of durability, the wall is probably half the thickness it should be. Moreover, as mentioned previously, it was constructed without the benefit of mechanical compaction of the concrete. As a result, reinforcement has insufficient cover and the protection offered by the chemical make-up of the concrete has been dissipated by the unkind environment. Small pieces of concrete have become detached from the outer surface of the wall and are a potential hazard to the public. Over a period of many years the co-owners have attempted to keep the problem at bay by effecting localized repairs but the scale of the task and the cost of the major works involved have proved to be too great.

The upper floors of the building were evacuated in 1995 with only the ground floor and basement remaining in use. During the intervening period there has been a concerted effort from many quarters to prevent this example of early reinforced concrete or ferro-concrete from falling under the demolition hammer and various studies have been carried out to address the viability of repair to enable the building to be brought back into use.

Glasgow City Council and Historic Scotland have come together to provide a temporary respite for the building by funding the essential protective works and the Glasgow Preservation Trust has been selected to spearhead and coordinate a scheme for reinstatement.

A number of options have been examined to restore the structural integrity of the building, one of which involves reconstruction of the outer wall in its entirety to replicate the original design. In addition, some major structural work is also required to the basement to arrest the combined deterioration of the columns and retaining walls and to provide a watertight environment. It follows that major refurbishment or replacement of the services, fenestration, finishes etc. is required and it will be necessary to comply with current standards for insulation and other building control requirements. Although in a building of such age major repairs and upgrading of this kind may be difficult to effect, the design solution is possible and reconstruction of the façade is considered to be a feasible option.

Grant funding will be required from a number of sources for any scheme to proceed, but with the continued help and enthusiasm of all those who take the view that this example of architectural and engineering history must be preserved, the scaffolding may yet come down to expose Lion Chambers as it once was.

ACKNOWLEDGEMENTS

Bussell, M.N. The era of the proprietary reinforcing systems. *Proceedings of the Institution of Civil Engineers*, 1996.
Cusack, Patricia. Lion Chambers: A Glasgow Experiment.
The Builders' Journal, Concrete and Steel Supplement, 30 January 1907.

FIGURE 6
The Lion Chambers.

Glasgow City Chambers

The City Chambers, located in the centre of Glasgow, has been the headquarters of successive councils serving the City of Glasgow for more than one hundred years.

Designed by William Young and built at a total cost of £578,232 it was inaugurated on 22 August, 1888 by Queen Victoria.

Glasgow City Council, Land Services, Richmond Exchange, 20 Cadogan Street, Glasgow, G2 7AD

The Kibble and People's Palaces

BILL STUART

INTRODUCTION

This chapter examines two of Glasgow's unique historical buildings which were both constructed in the 19th century and which hold a special place in Glaswegians' affections.

The principal feature common to both buildings is that they are constructed principally from glass and whilst this is not uncommon in modern buildings, the use of glass in this scale was almost unique in the 19th century. Each building is described separately including the designs for each structure which were state of the art solutions for that time.

The Kibble is based on the development of arched domes and was designed and constructed at a time when the utilisation of filigree cast and wrought iron with glass was at the late peak of its development. It is also interesting that the structure was effectively based on a form of industrialised building, as the structural frame elements were mass produced and as many as were required could be incorporated in the building. These frames are manufactured from wrought iron and are supported internally on iron ring-beams and cast-iron columns. The properties of the materials used were maximised in the design and this is explored in more detail in the consideration of the Kibble building.

The Winter Garden at the People's Palace is essentially part of an exhibition hall, the main building is a museum reflecting the modern history of Glasgow. The Winter Garden in plan is an elongated rectangle with a semicircular end, and the whole structure is topped with a high-level barrel-vault roof. Steel is the principal structural material used for the roof arches which form the arch/barrel vault which has created a most interesting profile. Internal supports are provided by cast-iron columns. The design and construction of the People's Palace is described later.

Cast iron and glass are common to both palaces but the two differ in that the structure of the Kibble Palace uses wrought iron while the People's Palace has steel. The following table illustrates the relative properties of these metals. Cast iron is used principally for columns receiving direct loads and wrought iron and steel for structural members subject to tensile/flexural bending loads.

Table of Comparative Factors

Load effects and other properties

	Compression	Bending/tension	Weight	Durability
Cast iron	1.0	1.0	1	high
Wrought iron	0.6	3.3	1	high
Steel	1.3	7.0	1	medium/low

Durability was vitally important for these buildings and the treatments now available for the protection of steel structures were not then available.

This chapter is as much about the development of society in the 19th century as it is about building design and construction. Society was significantly different in the 19th century from that which exists today and the separate development of each of the buildings over a 25-year period reflects, in part, the values which prevailed at that time. Whatever the reasons behind the developments we have inherited two buildings of importance to the people of Glasgow and the West of Scotland which continue to offer something special to everyone.

People's Palace

BACKGROUND

The information board in the main entrance to the People's Palace explains that it was built as a cultural centre for the east end of Glasgow. Glasgow, which, at the end of the 19th century, was the most unhealthy area of the city with the highest level of deprivation. The facility was over thirty years in the making and was first considered about 1866 when the sum of £2500 was realised by the Glasgow Corporation from the sale of the old Bridgeton Bleaching Green, also in the east end of the city. This sum was deposited with the Clydesdale Bank of Glasgow to gain interest with the purpose of providing a museum and gallery for the area.

The majority of members of the Glasgow Corporation were successful businessmen, of a liberal persuasion, with a strong social conscience. The building of a museum in the east end was seen as part of Glasgow's programme of municipal provision. This suggestion for cultural provision was led by the Council, there being no apparent pressure by local citizens for such a facility. However it must be remembered that the average working week even at the end of the century was about 60 hours and the working classes had little free time or access to works of art to allow them to identify the lack of such provision.

The first recorded reference for the provision of a People's Palace appears to date from an address by Councillor Robert Crawford to the Ruskin Society of Glasgow in 1891. Robert Crawford was the chairman of the council's health committee dealing with hospitals, cleansing and sanitation and also chairman of the committee dealing with galleries and museums. He expressed the view that one function was a logical extension of the other since the corporation made provision for the physical wellbeing of Glaswegians then it should also have regard to their cultural needs! His address was wide ranging and offers us an interesting insight into the living conditions of ordinary citizens at that time and the position of manufacturing, design and the arts in society. He suggested that a concern of the city council should be the procurement and conservation of works of art for the public and the provision of art galleries which he saw as being essential for the cultural and technical education of the working classes. He contended that the nation's manufactured goods were, in comparison to the other growth areas in Europe, 'heavy and clumsy in form, harsh and inharmonious in colour and dull and spiritless in ornamental treatment and that our artisans were destitute of resource and ingenuity and lacked liberal training.' He went on to state that in his view such deficiencies would result in a loss to the country both in our home and export trade and the maintenance of the UK's commercial position could only be secured by the general creation of a better understanding of art and the diffusion of scientific and technical knowledge. It was his opinion that 'it is essential that Schools of Science and Art are fostered and encouraged and that Museums and Art Galleries be established [with the object of] the more intimate combining of the Arts and the Crafts'.

At this time in history Britain was the source of most of the world's manufactured goods, including significant exports to Germany, but the position was now changing. Europe and the USA were a growing source of well-designed and manufactured goods, increasingly for export. These concerns were further developed in the lecture and Robert Crawford concluded that 'there should be developed (in the east end) accommodation for a School of Art including a central promenade and a music room, a lecture hall and reception room with ample corridors and with space to display popular scientific apparatus and the latest wonders of electrical or other sciences, having no birds or animals in captivity but everything rare, natural, interesting and instructive with nothing to be vulgar or mean'. He suggested that such a facility should provide quietness, isolation, dignity and peace combined with variety, attraction and life – a People's Palace maintained with a people's dignity'.

FIGURE 1
General view with repair works in progress. December, 1998.

Art at this time commonly centred on the provision of establishments where paintings and sculpture could be viewed and musical recitals offered. Therefore the proposals for a People's Palace were radical and enlightened and reflected the liberal policies pursued by the Council. He further suggested that such a facility be used for special exhibitions and that art collections held in trust by central government be freely drawn upon. There is evidence to suggest that there was pressure to provide financial support for music and Crawford apparently saw this as a source of competition for the limited funds available for cultural investment. He addressed this issue by suggesting that music should have a fitting and important place in cultural awareness – important but not predominant, contributing but not all absorbing. His solution was that promenade concerts be held in the evening in a hall sufficiently isolated but as an integral part of the building provision for the east end. The facility should allow for the 'fullest enjoyment of pursuits without interference of enjoyment by others in other separate departments'. A final – and for the times very radical suggestion – was that any such provision be allowed to open on a Sunday if the citizens so wished. This matter would be discussed later when Sunday opening became a controversial issue.

Crawford's lecture was well received by members of the Ruskin Society and it was a significant milestone in the proposals to develop a People's Palace. Interestingly, a fairly clear brief as to building purpose and function had been set out by Crawford in his lecture, all three to four years before any designs or drawings were produced.

In the 1890s Glasgow was grappling with major problems of slum housing, poor sanitation affecting health, crime and widespread drunkenness, poverty and disease. Against this background, the provision of cultural facilities was a relatively low priority and the City Fathers continued to foster developments for a range of public works to improve living conditions in the city as a whole. Early forerunners such as the establishment of the Loch Katrine water supply and the establishment of the Glasgow tramway system were major jewels in the crown of Glasgow's achievements. The reasons for the apparent delays in the development of the museum for the East End when viewed against this background become more obvious.

Glasgow noted the construction of people's museums elsewhere in the consideration of its own development. In 1887 the People's Palace for East London had opened followed by the People's Palace in Bridport, Connecticut which was a centre for working women. In 1898 an opulent People's Palace was opened in Zurich incorporating a large pavilion, concert halls, covered and open terraces and restaurants overlooking the lake. However, this provision was designed principally to cater for the needs of the growing tourist industry in Switzerland.

These developments were not direct models for Glasgow, but there was a similarity in aim to the East London Palace – providing opportunities for the working classes to experience culture. The declared object of the London Palace was 'to create and scatter pleasure' and this combination of social and civil engineering was mirrored in the proposals for the People's Palace for Glasgow.

Also in Glasgow at this time was the People's Palace Music Hall off Watson Lane. Until 1890 it had been known as the New Star Theatre, from 1892 to 1897 as the People's Palace Music Hall, and then until 1950 as the Queen's Theatre. It is believed to have been demolished in the 1960s. It has been suggested that some prominent Glasgow citizens were directors of the theatre and were instrumental in having the name changed in 1897 immediately prior to the official opening of the civic People's Palace – surely not a coincidence ?

THE PALACE BUILDINGS

The buildings of the People's Palace consist of two combined but separate structures. The principal building has a frontage of 100 ft (30.5 m) and a depth of about 40 ft (12 m) and is three storeys high. The construction is of fairly traditional design and is finished in red sandstone quarried in Dumfriesshire. This building was designed to have rooms for recreation and reading at ground floor level with a museum on the first floor and display accommodation, principally for art, on the upper floors. The second structure is the Winter Garden, which with the Kibble Palace in the Botanic Gardens is the major conservatory type of building in Glasgow. The Winter Garden is 180 ft (54.9 m) long, 120 ft (36.6 m) wide and 60 ft (18.3 m) high and has a floor area of about 19,175 sq ft (1,781 sq m) of which some 75% is available for walking. This building incorporates an internal garden and is multi-functional with access to the garden through passages at ground floor level from the main building which also incorporates balconies from its upper floors to overlook the gardens..

The external facade of the main sandstone structure has allegorical figures by the 19th century sculptor Kellock Brown. These figures represent ship-building, mathematical science, painting, textile industry and a large central figure over the main entrance represents progress.

FIGURE 2
People's Palace.
Main entrance
with statues.

At the formal opening of the buildings in January 1898, Bailie Borland who was chairman of the special committee formed to oversee the public interest in the development of the work observed that the Palace would provide a facility to accommodate permanent collections (of art and science) which related to the history and development of the city. He advocated that special exhibitions be held where prizes might be offered for works of special excellence. The Winter Gardens were designed to house a range of events including musical performances for large audiences. Borland considered that the provision of a building to accommodate such a diverse range of activities was unique in Britain.

It is interesting to note how closely the outcome in 1898 compared with the general proposals first suggested by Robert Crawford in 1891.

DESIGN OF THE BUILDINGS

The museum part of the building was of traditional red sandstone design. The drawings were completed in early 1895 and those for the Winter Gardens were completed late in 1896 and immediately thereafter the whole project was offered for contract through competitive tendering. The design for the latter consists principally of cast iron, steel and glass and is rectilinear in shape, rather like a shoebox with a curved roof. It has been suggested that the shape of the building follows that of the inverted hull of Nelson's flagship the *Victory*. This may indeed be the case as examination of the building does bring to mind the hull shape of an early 19th century warship and further, the People's Palace site as a whole is within 200 m of Nelson's column on Glasgow Green. It also has the distinction of being the first memorial column in the UK to have been erected in Lord Nelson's honour.

The Winter Gardens structure is essentially based on a series of framed arches carried on cast-iron columns which are spaced at 64 ft (19.5 m) across the centre of the building. The arched frames are made up principally from angle, tee and flat bar steel sections in the form of open lattice frames. The effect is an elegant, airy, bright and spacious building which is striking both internally and externally and which fulfils its objective. The design recognises the relative characteristics of these different materials, for example cast iron is

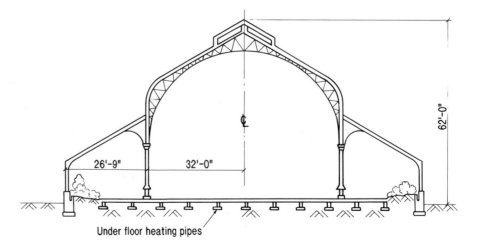

FIGURE 3
Cross-section of Winter Gardens. From original drawings 3rd December, 1896.

26'-9"   32'-0"   62'-0"

Under floor heating pipes

very good at carrying axial vertical loads in direct compression but weak if subjected to bending and was thus used for the columns. The steel sections are relatively light individually but when combined in the frames produce a structure that is very strong and capable of sustaining bending loads. A practical example of a compression type of load is that generated when a stack of bricks is placed on a steel plate. The load on the steel plate is compressive – pushing directly downwards. If we took the same load of bricks and hung them from the end of a steel beam then the major effect on the beam would be bending – rather like a fishing rod with a fish on the end. The steel frame used in the Winter Garden structure (Figure 4) is in the form of an arch which results in all bending loads being resolved into direct vertical compression loads carried directly onto the cast-iron columns. This design allowed best use to be made of the respective material properties. A further important consideration in using cast-iron columns was that these could be cast to a profiled shape which added elegance to the structure, something which could not have been readily achieved using steel sections.

A further unique feature of the design was a travelling ladder, constructed from steel sections similar to the main frame, which could move along the length of the building from the top of the column head to the peak of the arched roof. This provided access to the glazed roof and support frame for painting and general maintenance. Figure 4 shows a detail of the ladder and part of the arched frame.

The cast-iron columns were supported on concrete foundations and the whole structure was completed by the use of simple framed extensions spanning some 27 ft (8.2 m) from each side column to an external support wall, finished in sandstone, thus giving an overall building span of some 120 ft (36.6 m).

The Winter Garden was heated by an underfloor system comprising large suspended pipes, diameter 75 to 100 mm, which conveyed hot water along the length of the building. An underground boiler house was located at the end of the structure and spanned the building.

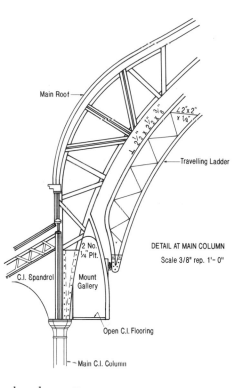

FIGURE 4
Detail at main column.

DESIGNERS AND CONTRACTUAL ARRANGEMENTS

The designer was A.B. Macdonald, a civil engineer and also the City Engineer. He was assisted by William Baird of the Temple Iron Works for elements of the Winter Garden framed structure. A.B. Macdonald was also responsible for a range of other significant projects in Glasgow including the public baths in Maryhill and in Springburn, the sewage works at Dalmuir and two of the bridges in Kelvingrove Park. His proposals for the museum portion of the Palace developed in the form of sketches from 1891 until final designs were completed in 1894. There was clearly a good deal of earnest discussion within the Council which resulted in a significant expansion of these outline proposals culminating in the addition of the Winter Gardens.

Tenders were invited in November 1894 for the museum project (originally called the East End Galleries and Recreation Rooms) and the contract for the main building works was awarded to Messrs Morrison & Muir at the

FIGURE 5
People's Palace.
General view with
repair works in
progress,
December, 1998.

approximate value of £12,300. Work commenced early in 1895. During the course of construction the contract for the Winter Gardens was awarded to Messrs James Boyd & Sons, Paisley who were well-established ironwork contractors. The value of the works was £7,200. It does however appear that the steelwork was supplied and erected by the Temple Iron Works.

The funding for the project was provided entirely by the City Council who had monies reserved from various sources:

Sale of Old Bridgeton Bleaching Green (including interest)	£ 3,900
Surplus (and interest) from the 1890 East End Exhibition	£ 2,800
Caledonian Railway	£ 8,200
Hunter Street Subway Fund (probable wayleave charges)	£ 7,000
Total	£ 21,900

It was not necessary for the Council to borrow money for the project and the balance of £2,400 was allocated for internal furnishings.

In 1896 the annual income for a skilled joiner/carpenter for a normal working week of 54 hours was about £90. Today that figure might be £11,000, for a week of 40 hours. On this basis the People's Palace would cost £2.5m – £3.0 m to build now.

The foundations created some difficulties due to poor ground conditions. The site is bounded by the River Clyde and the Camlachie burn, the latter in a buried culvert. To stabilise the ground the soft material would have been excavated to below the foundation level and then refilled with mixed stone to the level of the concrete foundations. A more sophisticated solution might have been used today but it is worthy of note that the buildings remain in use and have not shown any major signs of distress.

GENERAL COMMENTS

The building was opened as the People's Palace by Lord Roseberry on 22nd January 1898 who remarked that the building would be 'open to the people for ever and ever' and that it was 'a palace of pleasure and imagination around which the people may place their affections and which may give them a home on which their memory may rest'.

At the opening there were diverse exhibits on view, from paintings and sculptures to examples of decorative cast iron products from Walter McFarlane & Co. This company started trading in the 1850s with modest premises in Saracen Lane, off the Gallowgate and close to the Palace. In 1869 it had moved to Possil Park, where the company acquired a 'few acres' and established the Saracen Foundry which became famous throughout the world. The business closed in the 1970s although there remains to this day a Saracen Street in the district of Possilpark.

At a council meeting in December 1897, prior to the opening of the building, the vexed question of Sunday opening arose. A council proposal that both the People's Palace and the Kibble Palace should not be opened to the public on Sunday was overturned and thus the prophecy of Robert Crawford in 1891 had come full circle.

The *Glasgow Herald* noted at the opening that the People's Palace had been completed before the galleries in Kelvingrove and advised that 'residents of the west end must meanwhile repress their envy and possess their souls in patience until some years hence when the balance is adjusted by the opening of the splendid galleries at Kelvingrove'.

The relative uniqueness of the design of the People's Palace resulted in some difficulties in use. It was suggested that cross light in the museum caused a glare at the exhibition cases and made the contents difficult to view. To reduce this dazzle effect windows in the top floor were sealed and finished in matching sandstone which then prevented access to the external balustrade which in turn resulted in a reduced level of maintenance. The outcome was water penetration at roof level and a high degree of water absorption by the structural sandstone which resulted in a major outbreak of dry rot threatening the survival of the building in the 1970s.

Despite these drawbacks the People's Palace has been and continues to be a success and is a major part of Glasgow's culture. Since the late 1940s the main building has been transformed into a museum reflecting the local and contemporary history of Glasgow. At the present time the Winter Garden is under major repair following a fire in early 1998 and it is hoped that the building will be available for re-opening very soon.

Kibble Palace

BACKGROUND

The Kibble Palace in Glasgow's Botanic Gardens has a most unusual background, which in part reflects the history of Glasgow during the Victorian era. It was built by John Kibble, a native of Glasgow who spent a large part of his life in Coulport, a small village on Loch Long which is a sea loch on the Firth of Clyde 22 miles from Glasgow.

John Kibble was born in Glasgow in 1819 the son of a wealthy merchant. He had a most varied career as a metal merchant but described himself as an engineer. He was a man of many talents with an entrepreneurial flair and a range of interests including astronomy, photography, botany and the construction of glass houses. He is credited with the invention of a new method of ship propulsion for use on the Clyde which took the form of endless chain paddle floats, and as an experiment the steamer *Queen of Beauty* was thus equipped at Kibble's expense. Unfortunately, the trial was a dismal failure and the system was replaced by a steam engine designed by Robert Napier which was very successful.

However Kibble gained success with his photography. He invented a large glass plate camera which required to be mounted on a carriage and drawn by horses. This camera was said to produce photographs measuring 900 mm by 1100 mm of a perfection never before attained and his sun pictures gained him a gold medal at the International Exhibition in London in 1851 when he was only 32 years of age. It would seem he had both the time and the wealth during his working life to indulge his range of interests – not an unusual occurrence for gentlemen inventors in the Victorian era.

In 1810 Walter Nicol noted that 'a garden is not now reckoned to be complete without a greenhouse or conservatory with clear and fluid walls with light frames and lights'. The design of such structures continued and one of the leading designers of large greenhouses, J.C. Louden, enthused in an 1817

FIGURE 6
Kibble Palace,
general view.

publication about Victorian man's ability to 'produce summer in winter' and to 'command nature'. He was an innovative designer and advocated the use of ridge and furrow type glazing which he suggested enabled the sun's rays to be captured at two meridians instead of only one as was the case for flat glass. The sun's rays, being perpendicular to a glass face, will only have maximum concentration on a flat horizontal glass surface once per day, for example at noon. If, however, two plates are erected to resemble the roof of a house, then the sun's rays can impact twice per day, once on each face. This would be particularly effective if a greenhouse were constructed such that the roof faces were oriented to the sun's track on an east-west line. Louden was later to suggest that ridge and furrow construction be used for vast areas, an idea that was later to influence Sir Joseph Paxton, the designer of the Crystal Palace in London. Louden was also an avid supporter of the use of iron whilst other designers/ constructers of greenhouses still used wood. He is also credited, in 1816, with the invention of the wrought iron glazing bar which could be heated and drawn through a mould to the desired curvature which opened up a new dimension in curvilinear glasshouse construction. This was another development which due to the curved shape of the glass frame served to maximise the concentration of the sun's rays.

The method of producing curved wrought iron bars effectively replaced profiled bars made up from several short straight pieces of cast iron joined together to form an approximate arch shape. The other benefit was greater strength which helped improve the integrity of the overall arch construction favoured for single structure greenhouses or winter gardens. In 1818 Louden transferred all of his design rights to the company he worked for, W. & D. Bailey, who went on to produce many elegant conservatories. This form of design appears to have been admired by Kibble who adopted the principles when he came to consider the construction of his own palace.

John Kibble retired in 1865 to his house in Coulport at the relatively early age of 46 and apparently in good health. He turned his attention to leisure interests and is reputed to have designed his own private conservatory for his house at Coulport. It was, according to newspaper reports, an impressive curvilinear building housing a range of exotic plants with an internal water display. The conservatory consisted of a small dome and a large overarching dome constructed from shaped wrought-iron glazing bars and the whole structure was supported on 12 cast-iron columns. It was claimed that Kibble was influenced by the design of the Crystal Palace but his pursuit of glass building construction also reflected what was a wide and growing interest in the mid-19th century.

A daily newspaper in 1866 described Kibble's conservatory in the most glowing terms 'leaving the entrance apartment [the smaller entrance dome] we enter a great circular area which most fitly completes the picture. The overarching glass dome is supported by 12 fluted columns on a circular base of fretwork finished in the Moorish style and the whole interior is done up in white and gold. We have a circular fountain, in the centre of which is a romantic-looking island, studded with rocks and models of the most famous ruins in Greece and Rome. Two or three model ships are riding quietly in the island harbour and a tug steamer about 15 inches [430 mm] in length with

FIGURE 7
John Kibble
caricature. *The Baillie*, 12th November, 1873.

machinery and everything complete, may be seen hauling a vessel round the circle or into port as the case may be. Around the walls are fifty life-size statues [these were in fact plaster reproductions – although this was not reported in the newspaper] after the greatest masters including the Venus de Medici, The Greek Slave, Canova's Three Graces all standing lifelike amid shrubs and flowers from every part of the Globe'.

OF MATTERS BOTANICAL

The Royal Botanical Society of Glasgow was formed about 1817 reflecting the growing interest in tropical plants. The first Botanic Gardens were established on ground located between Dumbarton Road and Sauchiehall Road (as it was then called) generally where Fitzroy Place now stands and close to Charing Cross in Glasgow. An early director and supporter of the society was the famous botanist Sir William Hooker who was to leave Glasgow in 1841 to become the Director of the Royal Botanic Gardens at Kew.

After 20 years or so it became evident that due to the extension of the city and the gradual encroachment of housing another site was required. This was achieved about 1841 when the Gardens were moved further westwards to their present location. Originally the site occupied about 21.5 acres (8.7 ha) but around 1887 the area was extended to 40 acres (16.2 ha) the size of the park today. The Botanical Society was in effect a private club supported by the middle class in Glasgow and open only to paying members, although it was noted that the public was eventually allowed entrance on a Saturday for an entrance fee of one shilling (5p, equivalent to £7 today). It is important to understand the structure of the Botanical Society at that time and the part the Society had to play in relation to the establishment of the Kibble Palace in the Botanic Park Gardens.

John Kibble's family showed little interest in his conservatory and in 1871 he proposed to the Corporation of Glasgow that the whole structure be dismantled and re-erected in Queen's Park in Glasgow. Over the years it has been variously reported that the Palace was gifted to the people of Glasgow by Kibble but this was not the case. Kibble suggested to the Corporation that at his expense (£4500; about £650,000 today) he would considerably enlarge his iron and glass palace and transport and re-erect the whole structure in Queen's Park as a crystal palace which could accommodate 5,000 people under each of its two domes. However, he also stipulated that this should be in part a commercial venture and that he should receive a free site rental for a period of 20 years, that the income from the building be shared for certain events and that he would also operate and let the building for functions such as concerts. At the end of the 20 year period the Palace would, at no cost, be handed over to the Corporation 'to become the property of the citizens of Glasgow for ever and ever'. It is understandable how over time the myth of the free gift has grown. It appears from newspaper reports at the time that 'public opinion' was favourable, although it does not appear that the stipulations by Kibble were either fully known or reported by the press. The Corporation was made up largely of hard-headed business men who took their civic duties and stewardship of public funds seriously and after due consideration rejected Kibble's proposals. However, he was not put off by this setback and similar proposals to the Botanical Society were eventually accepted although it was noted that some members had misgivings.

Following completion in 1873, the new Kibble Art Crystal Palace as it was described seems to have been a success. It was opened on 20th June to a capacity audience of about 4,500 with a promenade concert and an address by John Kibble in which he spoke out against the evils of smoking and drinking (the Palace was not to be a venue for either activity during his management). Once again we witness his flair for showmanship with the provision of a large ornamental pond in the centre of the large dome which could be boarded over to accommodate orchestras or entertainers. 600 gas jets were also installed at a time when most houses were lit by candles. During the next few years the Palace was host to a number of significant events in addition to a programme of concerts held every Wednesday and Saturday evening. It became established on the social calendar of Glasgow and was used for art displays and meetings including the inaugural meeting of the British Association's Scottish Branch in September 1876. The inaugural addresses of the rectors of Glasgow University (Disraeli in November 1873 and Gladstone in December 1879) also took place in the Kibble Palace. However, the initial success did not continue which added to the financial problems the Botanical Society were experiencing. Between 1878 and 1881 the minutes of both the Society and the Corporation indicate that all was not well between John Kibble and the Botanical Society. The outcome was that in 1881 the Corporation advanced, through a guaranteed bond, sufficient monies to the Botanical Society to allow the purchase of the Palace and the remainder of the lease of the building, which still had 12 years to run. The Society had already obtained a loan from the Corporation to assist with the development of the gardens. The Directors of

FIGURE 8
D.L. Moody preaching in the Botanic Gardens, 1873 or 74.

the Botanic Gardens were obliged to obtain further loans from the Corporation to support development work and later found they were unable to repay the monies. This ultimately led to the Gardens being acquired by the Corporation as a park for the people of Glasgow and later land acquisition doubled the area of the park to its present size.

The purchase price from John Kibble was about £11,000 in 1881. He had expended £15,500 in total for the buildings sited in the Botanic Gardens, including his original costs for the earlier 'palace' at Coulport. From 1873 he had obtained income from organised events and letting of the Palace and since he had no rent to pay, it is likely that he made a modest profit.

John Kibble disappeared from the scene in 1881 and later moved to Cheshire where he lived until his death in 1894. The house at Coulport left the Kibble family and was eventually purchased by the Royal Navy in 1964, and later demolished to make way for a new Naval housing development. The late owner would however be gratified to know that one of the roads in the development is called Kibble Terrace.

After the Botanical Society acquired the Palace the building was cleared (including the plaster statues which had been transferred from Coulport) and then laid out as a winter garden. A new heating system was installed reportedly involving the installation of 3 miles (5 km) of copper piping. Thereafter the Palace was used only as a winter garden but in 1887, due to the Society's heavy debts the Gardens and Palace were acquired by the City as a public park. The Kibble Palace continues to be used as a Winter Garden and the statues now on display are of marble.

FIGURE 9
Kibble Palace.
Main dome from
connecting corridor.

DESIGN AND CONSTRUCTION OF THE PALACE

As noted the design of the original conservatory at Coulport was undertaken by John Kibble utilizing the principles of J.C. Louden. It was dismantled and brought up the River Clyde (then the River Kelvin) and offloaded close to its present location. It was considerably extended, as proposed by Kibble, with the manufacture and erection undertaken by James Boyd of Paisley, who incidentally was later to be involved with part of the construction of the Winter Gardens at the People's Palace at Glasgow Green.

The extended building form has impressive dimensions with a main dome of 146 ft (44.5 m) diameter and 43 ft (13.1 m) high and a small dome of 50 ft (15.3 m) diameter and 34 ft (10.4 m) high. The domes are connected by a vaulted corridor 40 ft by 28 ft (12.2 m by 8.5 m) the smaller dome having side transepts of 50 ft (15.3 m) on each side, each 28 ft (8.5 m) wide which results in an overall frontage of 150 ft (45.7 m). The total usable floor area extends to 23,000 sq ft (2,135 sq m) and in plan, from a bird's eye view, the Palace has a shape which is not unlike that of the starship *Enterprise* of Star Trek fame. For such a large building there is a considerable sense of space and lightness and with the range of exotic plants which are permanently on display there is a great sense of peace within the Palace. The early work of Louden was independently supported by Sir George Mackenzie creating a strong case for the utilisation of large-span lightweight structures provided the glazing would last and not suffer distress. Louden found that the glazing pane available in the early 19th century was capable of sustaining a horizontal shear load and so provide stiffening to the glazing bars. He had observed during the construction of a wrought iron dome that 'as the iron frame was erected, before it was glazed, the slightest wind could set the dome in motion from ground to apex... as soon as the glass was fitted it stood completely firm and rigid'.

It was daring to produce a structure of this type in which glass apparently took on an essential strengthening function in what was a discontinuous light shell structure (discontinuous because the frame structures are carried in part on ring beams and columns as described later). The glazing is not rigidly fixed, but set in glazing frames made of relatively lightweight wrought-iron bars with the space frames being mass-produced by James Boyd & Co., Paisley. This was state of the art construction for glass houses and the standardisation of the frames resulted in a building which could be dismantled for re-erection elsewhere. This no doubt reflected the thinking of John Kibble.

The overarching central dome (part of the larger flat dome) rests on an elevated fabricated iron ring beam which in turn is supported on a ring of 12 fluted cast iron columns. A further outer ring of 24 similar columns supports the main dome again utilising a ring beam to transmit the loads from the dome/arch onto the columns. At the top of each column a cast-iron filigree spandrel connects between the underside of the ring beam and the column. Whilst in appearance this is mainly decorative it is also structurally effective as it enhances the structure stability by stiffening the head of the column/ring beam connection. The smaller dome, forming part of the entrance, is of a similar construction but due to its much smaller size the construction is simpler with the dome being a semi-circle resting on a wrought iron ring beam which in turn is supported by six cast-iron fluted columns.

FIGURE 10
Kibble Palace.
Internal columns,
ring beams
and filigree
spandrels.

FIGURE 11
Entrance to Kibble
Palace, looking out.
(Courtesy of the
Glasgow Room,
Mitchell Library.)

The wrought iron side walls of both domes, the connecting corridor walls and transept walls are carried directly on to low level stone walls which has the effect of spreading the load of the structure fairly evenly around the building perimeter. In addition padstones are placed at right angles to the perimeter wall at about 4 ft (1.2 m) centres with filigree iron brackets fixed from the top of these pads at right angles to the structure walls. This has the effect of assisting with the spread of the load and also in providing stability to the building – not unlike the spandrel connections used with the columns. These brackets act in a similar fashion to the support stays which might be used to support a garden fence. If the fence is erected in a long line without being braced at 90° to the fence line, it will most likely fall over, especially under windy conditions. If, however, timber stays are installed at right angles to the fence line this has the effect of stiffening the wall, the wobble disappears and the wall is likely to stand up even under windy conditions.

The Kibble Palace is now almost 130 years old and despite the vast area of glass there has been very little wind breakage and indeed glass breakage on the Palace is much less than that experienced with the standard greenhouses at the park. The shape of the building probably offers less wind resistance allowing the wind to pass over the structure more readily. There has been some deformation of the main dome apparently caused by rotation of the support ribs. This movement, which has also involved the rotation of the glass panes in the sashes, has been accommodated by the slack in the glazing fit and has not endangered the structure in any way. This condition, which can be observed from within the building, is monitored by the Property Services Department of Glasgow City Council whose engineers are examining what remedial measures may be required to ensure that the Kibble Palace remains an inheritance for the people of Glasgow 'for ever and ever'.

FIGURE 12
Kibble Palace.
External wall
brackets and
wall foundation.

Princes Square, Glasgow

The highly prestigious and innovative redevelopment of a courtyard dating from 1841. Ove Arup & Partners Scotland were the consulting engineers to the project which subsequently received five awards or commendations from a variety of organisations concerned with the built environment.

Photograph: Alistair Hunter Photography

Ove Arup & Partners Scotland, Scotstoun House, South Queensferry,
West Lothian EH30 9SE

The Scottish Exhibition & Conference Centre
– including the former Queen's Dock and Finnieston Crane

NEIL BUCHANAN

QUEEN'S DOCK

The Scottish Exhibition and Conference Centre which was opened in 1985 is located on the site of the former Queen's Dock. The history of Queen's Dock is an interesting story in itself.

The Clyde Navigation Trustees bought 14 hectares of lands at Stobcross and Overnewton on the north side of the River Clyde in 1845. At that time it was planned to create 7 hectares of water space enclosed behind a gate with 540 metres of quay for the outer dock and 1250 metres of quay in the inner dock at a cost of £354,000.

In 1869 a new scheme which required the purchase of additional land was adopted by the Trustees. This provided for a tidal water area of 11 hectares estimated to cost £935,000 and to take 16 years to complete.

Work at Stobcross began with the the diversion of Pointhouse Road and the clearance of the timber yards, cotton mill and market garden, which occupied the site. The road works involved excavation of 230,000 cubic metres of sand, gravel and boulder clay and construction of a 12-metre high stone-retaining wall to the railway above. The diversion took three years to complete due to difficulties of the work and the bankruptcy of the appointed contractor.

The construction of Queen's Dock began in 1872, the first section of work including the entrance and turning basin. In 1876 two further sections of work were started, the western halves and the eastern halves of the two parallel basins. The costs of the work amounted to £527,000.

Investigation of the soils under the site had shown that the quay walls would in part be founded on stiff boulder clay but the centre and south quays would be located over sands, gravels and silt up to 24 metres deep. Normal foundations of wooden piles were unsuitable for such ground conditions but at that time cylinder foundations were being used in the construction of a new railway bridge across the River Clyde (the St Enoch Railway Station bridge). After trial construction of the quay walls using cylinder foundations, trenches were excavated for the quay walls to 1.2 metres below low water level and groups of triple interlocking cylinders of concrete rings cast on site were placed in the trenches. The cylinders were built to a height of 8.5 metres and then sunk by excavating sand and gravel from all three cylinders and adding weight of 305 to 406 tonnes on top of the cylinders. When the cylinders were sunk to

15 metres feet below quay surface level they were filled with concrete and sand. Walls of concrete blocks were then constructed on the cylindrical foundations and faced with sandstone from the Giffnock Quarries. When the walls were completed the landward side of the trench was backfilled and the water side excavated by hand to low water level and then by dredgers. The last copestone was inscribed and placed in 1880.

A 55-metre long swing bridge was constructed to span the 30-metre wide entrance. A hydraulic power station used a 75 hp compound steam engine to provide hydraulic power at a mains water pressure of 600psi to the swing bridge and cranes.

The hydraulic cranes were replaced by electric cranes on the north quay in the 1920s and on the south and centre quays in the 1950s.

The completed Queen's Dock involved the excavation and dredging of 2,180,000 cubic metres (4 million tons) of soils, the construction of 3,040 metres of quay wall and a total water area of 14 hectares (equivalent to 20 Hampden football pitches).

FIGURE 1
Placing of inter-locking cylinders of concrete rings.

FIGURE 2
Excavating from cylinders which are weighted.

Stobcross Quay which was constructed on the river front as an integral part of the Queen's Dock development was completed in 1882, extending to 910 metres (½ mile) in length.

The north quay originally handled coal and minerals while the centre and south quays handled general cargo trade. The sheds on the centre and south quays were of unimposing single storey brick construction.

FIGURE 3
Construction of
the walls.

FIGURE 4
Vessels used in
dredging the outer
basin.

FIGURE 5
Queen's Dock –
crane loading coal.

FINNIESTON CRANE

At the east end of the Stobcross Quay stands the Finnieston crane. The original 132-tonne crane was replaced in 1932 by the 178-tonne crane presently standing between the access road into the SECC and the River Clyde. This crane, the largest in the upper reaches of the Clyde, is of the hammerhead cantilever type, the overall height being 53 metres and the horizontal jib 46 metres long. The crane is powered electrically and the operator accesses his cabin by means of an electric lift located within the crane's support structure.

FIGURE 6
Finnieston Crane with straw train.

The crane was used to lift railway locomotives onto ships to be transported across the world as well as fitting engines and boilers into new Clyde-built ships. The crane continued to be used to load ships until the end of the 1980s. It is still a major landmark and from time to time has been used to support artistic features such as sculptor George Wyllie's straw locomotive and paper boat as well as advertising features such as cars during the Scottish Motor Show.

INFILLING OF QUEEN'S DOCK

The City of Glasgow acquired Queen's Dock from Clyde Port Authority in 1976 and commenced infilling late in 1977. The City restricted infilling to essentially demolition material which was end-tipped into the north and south basins. Because of the diverse nature of demolition materials and in particular the presence of timber, a boom was placed in the basins beyond the tip face to trap floating timber which was collected and burned on the quayside.

Much of the demolition material which was placed in the north basin came from the St Enoch Station and Hotel which were demolished in 1978.

The Gothic hotel which had opened in 1879 was a well-known landmark standing six storeys above the elevated railway station and extending to three floor levels below. The accommodation of the hotel was described in 1880 as 'over 200 bedrooms, 22 private and 20 public rooms not counting the restaurants and 45 servants apartments'. The railway station was built to provide platforms seven metres above street level, enabling the trains to cross the River Clyde at a height which allowed navigation on the river.

The station platforms were supported on brick arches which when demolished were extremely hard and difficult to break up. Other than the size of material tipped into the north basin at Queen's Dock, these materials were ideal fill. The demolition materials tipped in the south basin were generally

FIGURE 7
Finnieston Crane
with paper boat.

FIGURE 8
St Enoch hotel.

from tenement properties and were therefore smaller in size and had a higher timber content.

During the infilling period, two engineers of the City of Glasgow Department of Architecture and Related Services reported seeing a seal basking on a large piece of floating timber. This represented no small success in the cleaning up of the River Clyde which for many years was very polluted in the area of Glasgow – so much so that anyone falling in had to have their stomach pumped out.

The end tipping method of filling the two basins caused river silt in Queen's Dock to be displaced as a silt wave in advance of the tipped face. Site investigation indicated that there was little depth of silt trapped beneath the demolition fill. However, Clyde Port Authority would not permit the silt wave to be displaced into the river channel and at a later stage Clyde Port removed much of the silt displaced into the canting (turning) basin using a bucket dredger, whereupon the dock entrance was closed. When further filling progressed to the west quay wall of the canting basin the trapped silt was excavated, loaded into hoppers and removed.

THE SCOTTISH EXHIBITION AND CONFERENCE CENTRE

The nature of the ground at Queen's Dock presented difficulties for foundation support to the new SECC development because of the mix of rigid quay walls, loose sands and soft clays behind the quay walls and uncompacted and very varied demolition fill to the basins. After extensive investigation and testing it was decided to improve the ground by dynamic compaction techniques, simply by dropping a heavy weight on the ground to compress the granular soils to a state suitable to carry floor and structural loads. There was an area

FIGURE 9
The entrance to the Scottish Exhibition & Conference Centre.

FIGURE 10
Structural steel
being erected at
the SECC site.

where soft clay soils were not suitable for dynamic compaction and this was dealt with by removing the clay, replacing it with granular material and compacting that material by using another ground improvement technique commonly called vibrocompaction. Basically this system involves sinking a heavy vibrating poker into the granular material causing its densification.

The area of the new SECC buildings and an area to the west planned for a future extension were treated, approximately 33,000 square metres in total (or five Hampden football pitches).

The original design brief sought to provide two large halls of 10,000 and 4,500 square metres floor area without columns, and three smaller halls of 2,500, 2,000 and 1,000 square metres floor area. It was intended that the SECC should be suitable for a wide range of uses and built within a budget cost fixed by the funding institutions.

As built the SECC complex consisted of a complex of three separate buildings, a central concourse structure providing access to five exhibition halls and associated facilities. North of the concourse are two large halls located in a building 82.5 metres wide and 195 metres long, while on south of the concourse three smaller halls are located in a building 52.5 metres wide and 115.75 metres long.

The structural form of the two buildings on either side of the concourse comprises trusses supported by columns with rigid connections between the columns and their foundations and simple pin connections between the columns and the trusses.

Factors considered in determining this structural form were the need for column-free exhibition spaces, relative tolerance of differential settlement, accommodation of large heating and ventilation plant within the roof space and avoidance of flat-roofed construction. The loadings which each truss was designed to carry were 35 tonnes from services, 55 tonnes from the roofing and the trusses themselves and 46 tonnes snowloading.

The concourse structure of welded tubular steel lattice frame supports patent glazing and within the large space there are two 3-storey concrete structures accommodating offices, plant rooms and seminar areas.

FIGURE 11
The SECC
concourse.

Under the floors of the exhibition halls is a regular layout of 1760 metres of trenches containing underfloor services including water, electricity, telephone, compressed air and drainage. The trenches are served from a 335-metre long tunnel which runs the length of the concourse. The tunnel itself is a 3-metre diameter steel corrugated pipe with access chambers at each end.

The cost of the buildings including services was £31.67 million. The construction was funded by Strathclyde Regional Council, Glasgow District Council, Scottish Development Agency and a number of major financial institutions.

The SECC has provided for a wide variety of uses since its opening in 1985 including: Royal Scottish National Orchestra concerts, performances in the largest hall by Pavarotti and other international singers, ice dance shows, ballet, opera, pop concerts – as well as the circus and carnival, the Scottish Motor Show, the Scottish Modern Homes Exhibition and many other exhibitions and conferences.

The circus presented an interesting problem for the Halls' designer because it had been reported that elephants' urine was very acidic and damaged concrete with which it came into contact. After thorough research it was found that good quality concrete would be unaffected and the SECC's vast floor area was safe!

A major factor in choosing the former Queen's Dock site for the new SECC was its proximity to major transport connections and space available for large parking requirements.

Queen's Dock is adjacent to the Clydeside Expressway, built on the line of the Pointhouse Road which had been constructed in the 1870s. Finnieston Street, located to the east of Queen's Dock had a major junction with the

FIGURE 12
The SECC service tunnel.

FIGURE 13
An aerial view of the SECC.

Expressway including sliproads and traffic light control. There were therefore very good connections with the Expressway to the centre of Glasgow and to the west of Glasgow and the Clyde Tunnel. The Expressway at its east end provided connections to and from the M8 ring road which allows access north and south of the River Clyde but more importantly, motorway or dual carriageway to Greenock in the west and Edinburgh in the east.

The M8 connection provides a short ten minute journey to Glasgow Airport, a 30 minute journey to Prestwick Airport and a 50 minute journey to Edinburgh Airport. Local railway commuter transport is available at Finnieston Station immediately to the north of the Clydeside Expressway. This provided rail connections direct to Helensburgh and Loch Lomond in the west and Lanarkshire in the east. Within a distance of 1½ miles are Glasgow's two major Victorian railway stations which connect to the rest of Scotland and England.

Pedestrian access to the Finnieston Station is by way of a covered walkway from the main east entrance to the SECC concourse rising over the Clydeside Expressway and the electrified railway. The railway station was modernised to accommodate passenger traffic for SECC, including installation of a lift from road level to platform level. The elevated walkway was designed as precast columns with precast beams spanning between and transparent polycarbonate sheeting cover. The precast solution was adopted to enable fast and safe construction over the Expressway which was a major route in and out of Glasgow, usually operating at full capacity during peak hours. Also, because of overhead electricity cables, the railway line required working to strict safety requirements, including restrictions such as short possessions i.e. short periods when the electricity was cut off and the contractor had possession of the site. A concern in the design of the walkway was that because of its length (400 metres) and enclosure, it could behave like a wind tunnel. This problem did not arise, probably because of the doors at each end, but possibly also because of there being two sharp turns in the route of the walkway. The slope to rise above the Expressway required to be gradual to ensure that wheelchairs could use it safely without risk of 'running away'.

FIGURE 14
The elevated pedestrian walkway to the railway station.

A most unexpected event occurred during the installation of piles for a column to the elevated walkway. During driving of a precast pile, the operators heard running water. As part of any construction contract a search is made for information concerning existing services below the ground. It was discovered that the pile had been driven through a large storm-water sewer which was not shown in that location in any of the records obtained. Special cameras put down boreholes confirmed that the pile had penetrated the crown of the sewer pipe and had penetrated the invert (i.e. the floor). After repairs, further piles were driven in positions which avoided the sewer.

To assess parking requirements the types of events expected were analysed. These ranged from minor exhibitions with an attendance of 5,000 on 166 weekdays per year to major events with 25,000 attendance on 16 weekdays per year and spectator events with attendance of 10,000.

The various modes of travel were examined to assess usage of car, train, public bus service and hired coaches. The provisions made provided more than 3500 parking spaces for cars, coaches, taxis and commercial vehicles plus facilities for exhibition vehicles.

The very large areas of car parking presented a problem when the cost of surfacing was considered within the budget cost for the whole project. The surfacing finally adopted was an open textured 'bitmac' which allowed surface water to drain through to the underlying soils. The only real concern arising out of the use of such surface material was that women with high-heeled shoes might have difficulty in walking across the car parks. This was in part dealt with by using a finer stone on the roadways within the car parks.

The internal roads were built to high standards to enable fast access into and out of the car parks both east and west of the SECC buildings complex and as part of the traffic flow measures a low bridge carried traffic to the west car parks over a car only access to the east car parks. At the time of redeveloping the SECC site to coincide with the building of a new conference hall in 1997, the whole traffic scheme was altered with the benefit of over 10 years experience. The alterations included demolition of the low overbridge and creation of a new road layout at ground level.

There is also mooring available on the 750-metre long river quay wall and pontoons have been placed against the river quay for the use of small vessels. A ferry service did in fact operate on the stretch of the river between St Enoch and Govan during 1988, the year of the National Garden Festival which was held in the former Prince's Dock site across the river from the SECC.

Another factor in favour of the SECC being located at Queen's Dock in Glasgow was the availability of hotels within a reasonable distance. At the time of its opening in 1985 the SECC could list a large number of hotels of at least 3-star quality – four within walking distance, 13 within 20 minutes travel, nine within 30 minutes travel and a further 33 hotels within 60 minutes travel.

From the early planning stage it had been envisaged that a hotel would be built at the Queen's Dock site but this did not happen until four years after the SECC opened in 1985 when the Moat Hotel (formerly the Forum Hotel) was opened. The hotel is a 20-storey structure totally clad in glazing. It is an imposing building but it has been remarked that there are few cities where such a high building would have been allowed on a river frontage.

At the very west end of the former Queen's Dock is the former hydraulic power station which was repaired and converted into a complex of three restaurants. Sadly the restaurants did not survive. One of the dining experiences in the river-facing restaurant was looking across the former entrance to Queen's Dock to Glasgow's helicopter pad. The helicopter operations there include private flying, Radio Clyde's 'spy in the sky' for traffic reports and the Strathclyde Police helicopter which with its video and infrared cameras is extensively used in searches for both criminals and missing persons.

The other old building standing in the area of the former Queen's Dock is the Rotunda. This brick structure originally was built over a terminal shaft providing access to the Harbour Tunnel which crossed under the River Clyde. The shaft contained stair access for pedestrians and a lift for horses and carts which drove through the tunnel.

The Rotunda was altered by infilling the shaft and constructing three floors of restaurants. The Rotunda structure on the south side of the River Clyde was used as a restaurant during the National Garden Festival in 1988.

After the opening of the SECC in 1985 and the hotel in 1989, the planned expansion of the SECC halls complex was carried out in 1997 by construction of a large hall at the west end of the building north of the concourse. The original buildings had been finished in red and grey colours which had been chosen by the architect to reflect the shipbuilding history of the River Clyde where of course all ships had first coats of red lead. An unkind description of the buildings in an architectural guide is 'red and grey wriggly metal glandular volumes flanking a central, top-lit atrium'. Glasgow people knew what was meant when reference was made to the 'red sheds' but the colour scheme was changed in 1997 to grey.

FIGURE 15
The Moat hotel, situated alongside the water.

FIGURE 16
The former hydraulic power station.

FIGURE 17
The former
hydraulic power
station.

The most spectacular change, however, in 1997 was the construction of a new conference hall at SECC which was designed by Sir Norman Foster, an architect of international reputation. This building, popularly known as the 'Armadillo', is the subject of another chapter.

BELL'S BRIDGE

It was always intended to connect the SECC site to the south side of the river but it was not until Glasgow was chosen for the third National Garden Festival to be held in 1988 that connecting the north and south sides of the river could be economically justified.

One alternative considered was to use one of the Harbour Tunnels but the cost of renovation and maintenance as well as doubts about the willingness of the public to use tunnels did not encourage the adoption of the tunnel access system. The preferred solution was a bridge crossing and the design brief required there to be a pedestrian crossing which would open to allow river traffic through and which could be removed and relocated to a preferred position after the 1988 Garden Festival.

The successful design was a balanced cable-stayed swing bridge pivoting on a central pier to give a 35-metre wide navigation channel in the river which reaches 120 metres in width. The 8-metre wide fully covered walkway is spectacularly elegant and won a number of awards.

The bridge is still located in its original site and has been used only on special occasions since 1988.

THE FLOOD OF 1996

The original River Clyde had many shallows and before the river became a commercial waterway cattle forded the river at Dumbarton.

The River Clyde has been altered over the course of the last 200 years to allow passage of large cargo and passenger vessels and newly-built vessels of all types and sizes including the *Queen Mary*, the *Queen Elizabeth*, the *QE2* and the last British battleship, the *Vanguard*, all of which were built in Clydebank to the west of Glasgow.

The manmade alterations included training of the river by walls and dykes and dredging to achieve depths of water to enable passage at all stage of the tide. With the demise of the Glasgow docks dredging has been considerably reduced. The river at Glasgow has thus become shallower, and together with the threat of rising sea levels because of global warming there is cause for very careful consideration to be given to the flood flows in the River Clyde.

A primary concern in the design of any development beside a river is the selection of ground floor levels whereby the risk of flood is acceptably low and the floor level of the SECC buildings complex was set at 5.1 metres above Ordnance Datum, 0.4 metres above the quay wall levels.

In December 1996 the SECC site was flooded. What happened was not caused directly by flood levels in the River Clyde. Due to exceptionally heavy rainfall in the catchment area of the River Kelvin, which meets the River Clyde downstream of the former Queen's Dock site, the River Kelvin overtopped its banks in the vicinity of Kelvinbridge Underground Station. The overflowing water entered a disused railway tunnel and emerged at Finnieston Railway Station before running across the SECC site and running off the site over the quay wall into the River Clyde. The SECC underground service tunnel was

FIGURE 18
Bell's Bridge.

flooded and the Fire Brigade helped deal with that problem. The service tunnel was cleaned and restored to working condition in a very short time. However, extensive damage was caused to the river quay wall, including movement of the wall which resulted in surface settlement behind the quay wall. Repairs were carried out to the quay wall.

This event was one which even with the benefit of hindsight could not have been predicted. Not only was the route of the flood water unexpected but the flood level of the River Kelvin on this occasion was 1.6 metres above the previous maximum.

FIGURE 19
The flood of 1996.
(Courtesy Mirror
Syndication
International)

Designers and builders

SECC	*Project Management*	*Bovis Construction Ltd*
	Architect	*James Parr & Partners*
	Civil & Structural Engineers	*Thorburn Associates*
	Building Services Consultants	*Hulley & Kirkwood*
Hotel	*Management Contractor*	*Rush & Tomkins*
	Architect	*Cobban & Lironi*
	Civil & Structural Engineers	*W A Fairhust & Partners*
Bell's Bridge	*Civil & Structural Engineers*	*Crouch & Hogg*
	Contractor	*Lilley Construction Ltd*
	Fabricator	*Sir William Arroll & Co.*
Armadillo	*Project Management*	*Bovis Construction Ltd*
	Architect	*Sir Norman Foster*
	Civil, Structural and Building Services Consultants	*Ove Arup & Partners*

REFERENCES

Berry, S., Whyte, H. (Eds.) *Glasgow Observed*, John Donald, 1987.

MacRae, G. Unpublished Technical Report, 1998.

McKean, C., Walker, D., Walker, F. *Central Glasgow* (an illustrated architectural guide), Mainstream Publications (Scotland), RIAS, 1989

Reid, W.M., Buchanan, N.W. *The Scottish Exhibition Centre*, (technical paper), Thomas Telford, 1987.

Riddell, J. *The Clyde*, Fairlie Press, 1988.

Riddell, J.F. *Clyde Navigation*, John Donald, 1979.

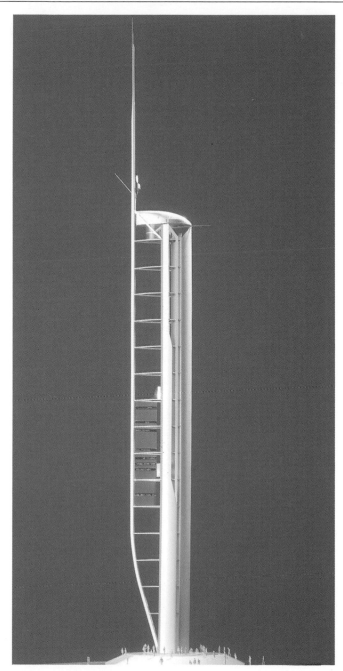

The Science Centre Tower

The Science Centre Tower is the first 100m high structure which is designed to be turned into the wind. The Tower will form a key exhibit at the Glasgow Science Centre and for this reason Buro Happold have designed all aspects of the engineering to be made as clear to view as possible: structure, access, services, communications and turning mechanisms.

Photograph courtesy of Buro Happold and Richard Horden Associates.

Buro Happold, 20–21 Woodside Place
Glasgow G3 7QF

Glasgow's Stadia

W.M. REID

Statistics show that Glasgow ranks about number 400 in the world in population. Statistics also indicate that it is unique for the number and quality of its major stadia. Glasgow can claim three of the finest stadia to be found anywhere in the world, at Celtic Park, Hampden and Ibrox.

Why should Glasgow find it necessary to have three world-class stadia? That it is passionate about football is clear, but it is not unique in this respect. What sets Glasgow apart is the intensity of the long-standing rivalry between Celtic and Rangers. Such are the feelings of the respective supporters towards each other, that neither Celtic Park nor Ibrox can be universally accepted as a neutral venue. These grounds are more than mere stadia, they are potent icons and are each seen as hostile territory to rival supporters, irrespective of which team may be competing on the playing surface.

The need for a neutral venue created a void which Hampden Park has filled for many years. It is the recognised Scottish Arena for major cup finals and international matches. Its association with the 'big occasion' has conferred on it an aura with fans and players alike that condemns all alternatives as second class.

The status of Glasgow's three major stadia has existed for many years. Before looking behind their current façades it is appropriate to make a brief review of the history and development of each ground.

Background and history

CELTIC PARK

When the first match at the current location of Celtic Park took place on 20 August 1892, the ground was described as the best in Britain. It was an immediate success and hosted its first international football match against England in 1894, when an attendance of 46,000 was recorded. The ground in its initial format was multipurpose, incorporating both a cinder running track and a concrete cycle track. The latter was used in 1897 to host the only World Cycling Championships ever to be held in Scotland. In 1928 Celtic Park hosted Scotland's first ever speedway race just one year before the opening of a new South Stand which cost £35,000 and provided 4,800 seats. At that time the capacity was approximately 85,000. This was less than Hampden and Ibrox, but more than any football ground in England.

No major development of Celtic Park took place in the years following the 1929 building of the South Stand, but notable works were the addition of floodlights in 1959 (described at the time as the tallest lighting masts in Britain); covering the West End (Celtic End) in 1957; re-roofing the North End (Jungle) in 1966; covering the East End (Rangers End) in 1968 (the year after they won the European Cup); seating of the paddock (3,900 seats) and re-roofing the South Stand in 1971; upgrading the South Stand accommodation and re-roofing the West Terrace in 1986. Apart from adding 5,033 seats to the North End (Jungle) in 1993 there were no other major alterations to the ground accommodation before the club moved to play at Hampden for the season 1994-95 when the first phase of the new Celtic Park began.

IBROX PARK

The current location of Ibrox Park on Edmiston Drive was opened to herald the new century on 30 December 1899. Rangers were flushed with success, having won the league the previous season without dropping a point.

The new Ibrox Park however, was destined to suffer misfortune. On 5 April 1902, with a crowd of 68,114 in the ground for an international match between Scotland and England, a rear section of a wooden terrace 'collapsed like a trap door' and caused 125 spectators to fall 50 ft to the ground below. Twenty-six spectators died and 500 were injured, including many who were crushed in the panic to escape from the area of collapse.

After this disaster, the ground was remodelled and by 1910 the ground capacity was 63,000 with solid earth embankments replacing the timber structures. At this point, Glasgow had the three largest purpose-built football stadia in the world. In 1929 the existing Main Stand (South) was opened. Designed by the eminent Scottish Engineer and Stadium builder, Archibald Leitch, it was the grandest stand yet seen in Britain. With a 10,000 seat capacity, its criss-cross decoration on the front of the balcony (still preserved to this day) together with the impressive red brick façade, it perhaps represented the pinnacle of Leitch's career.

The terracing continued to be expanded, and in 1939, 118,567 spectators watched a match against Celtic. This is a record for a league match in Britain. 1953 saw the introduction of floodlights at Ibrox, but it was not until 1966 that they were used for a league match against Queen of the South (which Rangers won 8-0).

Roofs were added to the terracing and by 1966 both the North and East were covered. In 1973, 9,600 bench seats were installed on the North Terracing and it was renamed the Centenary Stand.

Transformation of Ibrox Park into the modern stadium of today commenced on site in 1978, but not before its reputation as a world-famous venue was blighted by a further series of tragic events. In 1961, two fans died when a barrier failed; in 1967, eight injuries occurred at Stair 13 and this was followed by a further 24 injuries at the same location in 1969. Tragic though these events were, they were less serious than the horrendous events at the now notorious Stair 13 at the Old Firm game on 2 January 1971 – 66 people died and 145 were injured on that fateful day.

As a direct result of the disaster in 1971, a *Guide to Safety at Sports Grounds* was published in 1973 and the *Safety at Sports Grounds Act* was passed in Parliament in 1975. These formalised, for the first time, guidance on the safety of spectators and set minimum standards for designers and club administrators to follow.

HAMPDEN PARK

Hampden Park is the home of Queens Park Football Club. Queens Park is unique in the senior Scottish football leagues as being a wholly amateur football club. Although Queens Park is the oldest football club in Scotland, having been formed in 1867, Hampden, in its present location, is the youngest of Glasgow's three major stadia. The first match at Hampden took place in October 1903, when Queens Park played Celtic. The capacity of the ground at this time was 65,000.

Hampden initially had two 4000-seat stands on the South Side, with a pavilion in between. As Hampden became the favoured venue for international matches, the capacity was steadily increased. The Scotland v. England international of 1908 (see Figure 1) hosted 121,452 spectators (the match ended in a 1–1 draw, with Wilson scoring for Scotland and Windridge scoring for England). In 1923 additional land was purchased which created space for Lesser Hampden and for car parking space adjacent to the stadium. In 1927 an additional 25,000 spaces were added to the ground, and by 1937 the North Stand (seating 4,500) was complete. At this stage the official seated and standing spectator capacity at Hampden was 150,000 compared with 118,000 at Ibrox and 92,000 at Celtic Park.

By the mid 1930s Hampden had already hosted many international football matches, and had enjoyed a monopoly of all Scottish Cup Finals since 1925. From 1937 onwards virtually all Scottish senior team internationals were hosted at Hampden, with record attendance being a regular feature. The Scotland v. England fixture on 17 April 1937 attracted the highest crowd ever

International Football Match : Scotland v. England, Hampden Park, Glasgow, April 4, 1908

FIGURE 1
Hampden Park, Glasgow, 1908.

recorded in Britain of 149,415 (with at least another 10,000 reported as gatecrashers). The cup final of the same year between Celtic and Aberdeen also set a record for attendance at a match between two British clubs of 144,303 or 147,365, depending on the source of the information. Hampden can also claim the record for the highest attendance at a UEFA competition, when a semi-final between Leeds and Celtic attracted 136,505 in 1970.

In 1950 Hampden lost its title as the largest capacity stadium in the world when the Maracana Stadium in Brazil opened with a capacity of 200,000. By this time the permitted capacity of the stadium had been reduced to 135,000 and this process of reduction continued until by 1977 the official capacity was down to 81,000.

During the 1970s Hampden's future came under the microscope, and there were many false starts and disappointing reversals for those promoting its future as a top class national stadium. During the time of uncertainty, upgrading did take place. However, by March 1994 a new roof had been completed over the North and East terraces to give an all-seated stadium with a certificated capacity of 40,000 seats. In 1995 the future of Hampden was finally confirmed by the award of a £23m grant from the National Lottery Millennium Commission. This financial windfall, added to £28m raised from other sources, generated the finance to lift Hampden back into the position of being one of the world's finest sporting venues.

GLASGOW'S STADIA FOR THE NEW MILLENNIUM

By the dawn of the year 2000, Glasgow will boast three highly efficient football stadia, each of which will rank amongst the very best in the world. It would be simplistic, however, to regard the modern Ibrox, Celtic Park or Hampden as football grounds which exist only for match-day use. The reality is much more impressive. Each stadium hosts a large-scale commercial enterprise, providing full and part-time employment for hundreds of staff.

Restaurants, commercial offices, conference facilities, exhibition space, museums, retail outlets, merchandising etc. are all integral parts of club business plans to such an extent that ticket revenue may no longer represent even half of the financial income.

Although owners of the three stadia share a common objective to be major venues in the European and international scene, the three stadia are very different in structural form and internal layout. Each is distinctive and each has evolved from a different background. All three have been influenced by individual priorities which has generated the final product.

IBROX PARK

Following the 1971 disaster, Ibrox Park had the worst safety record in British football. Action was urgently required, and the Rangers Football Board responded to the challenge. Showing admirable courage and foresight, they rejected the concept of tinkering with the existing stadium and instead opted for a completely remodelled ground which would retain only the Main Stand which had given excellent service since it opened in 1929.

During the initial planning stages, Rangers were extremely fortunate in having a strong driving force in Willie Waddell as their General Manager.

Many of the fundamental decisions taken at the concept formulation stage were heavily influenced by his vision of the priorities for a modern football ground.

Some of the key features which he insisted upon were:

- **Proximity of the crowd to playing surface**
  'He (Willie Waddell) wanted the crowd close enough to smell the liniment'.
  Atmosphere was of paramount importance.

- **Good sight lines**
  There was no question in his mind that there should be any restricted viewing.

- **High quality pitch**
  The playing surface could not be compromised. The shading of the sun from the South Stand was not being altered, but he was concerned that lack of wind flow across the pitch would be damaging.

- **Excellent safety standards**
  With the previous safety record at Ibrox, creating a safe environment was his over-riding priority. Wide concourses, generous staircases and absence of fire sources were all basic requirements of his concept brief.

The above priorities, together with the need to incorporate commercial space for letting, were the basic parameters given to the design team. Very little relevant precedent was available to the Engineers and Architects (Thorburn & Partners and T.M. Miller & Partners respectively), and at that time the design guidance available was relatively basic.

For economy, ease of phasing and preservation of wind flow on the pitch, individual stands with open corners were chosen. The end stands (East and West) were designed with commercially viable office space integrated into the rear elevation such that they were totally independent of the primary spectator functions of the stand.

The construction work commenced in October 1978, with the clearing of the East Terrace and its replacement with the new Copland Road Stand. This exercise was repeated at the West end with the construction for the Broomloan Road Stand and, finally, at the North side with the removal of the Centenary Stand and its replacement with the Govan Stand. The new Ibrox was officially opened in September 1981, at which time the official capacity was 44,000. The extent of the achievement by Rangers in transforming their stadium cannot be overstated. There were no grants available to them, so the redevelopment had to be financed from their own resources.

Transforming the old Ibrox to a modern stadium (Figure 2) was a major triumph, but was to be only the first step in creating a dynamic commercial venue. Development of the space at the rear of the Govan Stand produced a high quality restaurant and hospitality area with boxes overlooking the pitch, together with additional club offices and hospitality space which had non-match day seminar and exhibition use. A new club deck above the Main Stand yielded an additional 7,300 seats with high quality concourse and hospitality

FIGURE 2
Aerial view of
Ibrox park in 1998.

facilities, while alteration to the seating layout of the original stands and infilling of the North East and North West corners raised the total capacity of the ground above 50,000 seats.

The structural form of the stands at Ibrox are all similar in that the roofs are supported on large trusses which span the full width of each stand supported by columns located at each gable. The trusses at either end span 78 metres, while the Govan Stand truss is 108 metres long, and the Main Stand extends to 145 metres, which at the time of construction made it the longest clear span girder of its type in the world. The form of the seating decks are identical in the Copland, Broomloan and Govan Stands, with two separate tiers accessed by spacious and generously provided concourses. The angle of slope of the lower tiers is 22°, and 28° in the upper tiers. The club deck of the Main Stand has an angle of 34°, which is the maximum recommended by the 1997 *Guide to Safety at Sports Grounds.*

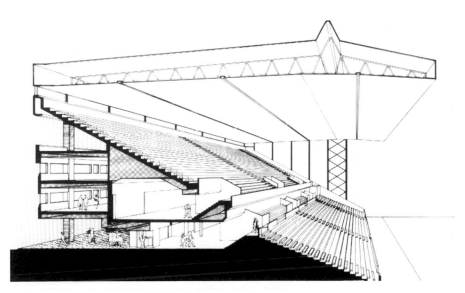

FIGURE 3
The Broomloan
Road West Stand
at Ibrox.

Figure 3 shows a cross-section of Broomloan Road Stand and illustrates the double cladding system adopted for the roof. This form of construction which encapsulates the roof steelwork is relatively expensive and is now rarely adopted in modern stadia designs.

A feature at Ibrox, not present at either Celtic Park or Hampden, is the large screens which are located at the North East and North West corners (see Figure 4). Accommodating the screens necessitated moving the columns which supported the large roof trusses and the introduction of heavy cantilever trusses to transfer the reactions at the end of the truss to a location which did not interrupt the sight lines. This work was completed in 1997. The complexity of the structural solution is, however, concealed by the cladding which covers the roof steelwork.

Ibrox was the first of the new generation of stadia in the UK. The standards set there in 1978 became a blueprint for others to follow in subsequent projects.

CELTIC PARK

While the development at Ibrox was the first complete stadium redevelopment, Celtic left it much later to transform their ground to meet the demands of modern standards.

The new Celtic Park (60,000 seats) has a larger spectator capacity than Ibrox (50,000). To put these in perspective, Celtic Park will enter the new millennium ranked about 10th in seated capacity terms in Europe, whilst Ibrox and Hampden will rank approximately 15th.

The scale of the East, North and West Stands dominates that of the original South Stand. If the ground is ever redeveloped to a uniform bowl by upgrading the South Stand, then the capacity could rise to nearer 75,000 seats.

Concealed within the new strands is a labyrinth of areas with potential for commercial exploitation for both match day and non-match day use. The philosophy behind this is similar to the strategy adopted and successfully executed at Ibrox – to maximise revenue generation from the stadium by non-match day activity. Celtic FC also have plans to exploit the stadium facilities and functions to generate redevelopment of the Parkhead district of Glasgow.

The design problems posed by the development of Celtic Park differ significantly from those at Ibrox, and this is reflected in the solutions adopted. Among the principal differences are:

• The ground at Celtic Park was vacated for a year while the first phase was constructed. Ibrox was in constant use throughout the construction phase.

- Access to the stand locations at Celtic Park was restricted by the proximity to the graveyard at the rear of the North Stand. At Ibrox there was relatively clear access around all the new stands.

- The scale of the new Main Stand at Celtic Park is disproportionate to that of the new East, West and North Stands, and this has resulted in relatively small scale corner stands at the South East and South West corners. At Ibrox, the corners at either side of the Main Stand (South) are open.

When the West Stand was completed in 1998, Celtic Park had a ground capacity of approximately 60,000 seated spectators, making it the largest in the UK.

The enclosed bowl format at Celtic Park is the classic arena shape which has proven to be the most popular with fans (see Figure 5). The bowl shape has, however, two potential drawbacks compared with the open corner solution. It does not provide the crowd segregation as with separate stands, and it also inhibits air circulation across the pitch. Pitch quality at Celtic Park is, however, enhanced by the relatively low South Stand which limits the extent of sun shading that would normally occur in a uniform 60,000 seat bowl stadium.

A typical cross-section of the East Stand at Celtic Park is shown in Figure 6. The cantilever roof is supported on a single column at the rear of the stand, which is in turn stabilised by the seating deck support structure. This is a relatively common configuration and variations on a similar theme can be seen at the grounds of Leeds United, Middlesbrough, Sunderland and others. The roof cladding is under-slung, which gives a clear, neat underside to the roof, but leaves the structural members exposed above. The benefits of this type of roof are that it prevents birds roosting above the seating deck, enhances acoustics, and allows easy maintenance of roof support structure and provides an access platform for roof-mounted plant. In common with most modern

FIGURE 5
The enclosed bowl shape of Celtic Park.

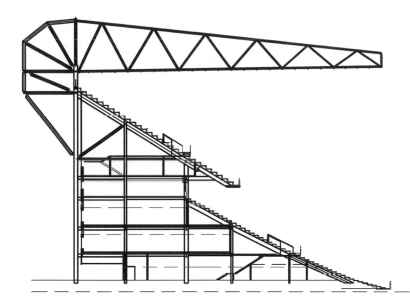

FIGURE 6
The East Stand
at Celtic Park.
(Courtesy of Percy
Johnson Marshall
& Partners.)

stadia, floodlights are no longer supported on large pylons, but are fitted to the front edge of the roof structure where they can be evenly distributed and readily maintained. The accommodation under the roof consists of seating decks, concourses, stairways, hospitality areas and other revenue-earning space. For ease and speed of construction the main frame comprises structural steel members, and the decks and floors are in precast concrete and composite *in situ* concrete respectively. A complication of the location of Celtic Park was that the area had been undermined by the extraction of coal in the 19th century and this had left voids in the underlying rock. This raised concern that subsidence might occur at some future time which could compromise the integrity of the foundations. To prevent damage to the stands by mining subsidence cement-based grout was pumped into the underlying voids prior to the installation of support piles. In all some 26,403 tons of grout were pumped into the ground at Celtic park prior to the commencement of the new stand construction. The maximum angle of slope of the seating decks at Celtic Park is 33º.

HAMPDEN PARK

The redevelopment at Hampden Park has been a phased transition from the old 1929 seated South Stand, together with standing terraces on the East, West and North, to a completely seated bowl stadium with an excellent modern Main South Stand. A feature of Hampden which belies its scale is the fact that the pitch is lower than the surrounding ground, 7-8 metres below the level of Somerville Drive in the North and 4 metres below the ground floor of the South Stand. This has the effect of reducing the impact of the structures and making them more compatible with the scale of the adjacent properties.

Figure 7 shows a cross-section of the South Stand. As at Celtic Park, the roof structure is of cantilever form but, in contrast, support is derived from two columns acting together to carry the compression and tension forces generated by the cantilever. The necessity for this structural form at Hampden can be seen in the cross-section of the North Stand (Figure 8) where there was

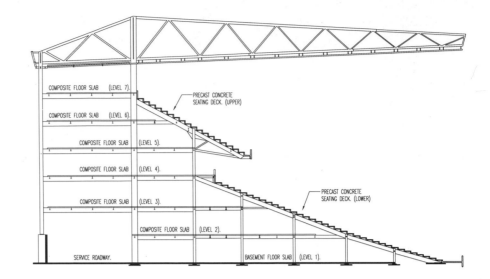

FIGURE 7
Hampden Park –
the South Stand

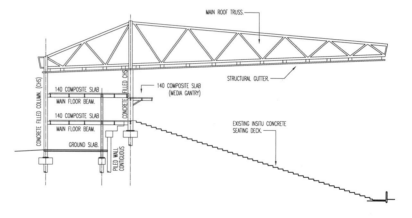

FIGURE 8
Hampden Park –
the North Stand

effectively very little seating deck structure available which could have been used to stabilise a single column solution.

The two rows of columns at the rear of the stands consists of circular steel tubes varying in diameter from 508 to 762 mm. These columns provide the vertical support for the roof, floors and the rear of the seating deck. In addition to providing vertical support, they are also required to accommodate lateral forces generated by spectator activity. When their movement is co-ordinated by music, spectators can induce significant dynamic downward and sway forces in the structure and particularly if the natural frequency of the stand (the rhythm at which it naturally vibrates) is synchronised with the beat of the music.

At Hampden Park the rear columns have been filled with concrete, which significantly increases both their strength and their stiffness.

The maximum angle of slope of the seating deck at Hampden is 29° at the rear. The completed Hampden stadium will accommodate some 52,500 spectators and have 72,000 sq metres of floor area. It will compare favourably

in standard with any similar facility and will restore Hampden Park to the leading position in the world of soccer stadia that it has occupied for the majority of its 100 years history. Figure 9 shows an aerial photograph of the completed stadium.

CONCLUDING REMARKS

The City of Glasgow possesses a unique character stemming from its people, their interests, their business acumen, their commercial skills and, perhaps most of all, their passion for football and sport in general. The City can claim to be of ancient origin, but modern in thought.

During the 20th century, Glasgow has staged many memorable spectacles on the playing surfaces of its three major stadia. The depth of passion for football, the rivalry between the major clubs, and the competition for the honour of hosting international and other prestigious matches has generated in the City a richness of stadia provision not exceeded anywhere else in the world.

As we enter the new millennium, there is no evidence of any diminution in the unique factors which have placed Glasgow at the forefront of stadia excellence. There is no doubt that Glasgwegians can now look forward to reaping the benefits from the investments which have been, and will continue to be made, by those responsible for the stewardship of some of the City's greatest assets.

PHOTOGRAPHS
Photographs of the Celtic and Rangers stadia are reproduced by kind permission of Rangers F.C. and Celtic F.C.

FIGURE 9
Aerial view of Hampden Park in 1999. (Courtesy of Austin Reilly, Manging Director, The National Stadium PLC, Hampden Park, Glasgow).

Celtic Park, Glasgow

Celtic Park, Glasgow is the largest club stadium in Britain with a capacity of over 60,000. The stadium has been developed on its existing site with three new stands on the north, east and west sides of the ground, complimenting the original 'new' stand developed in the 1970s.

Phases 2 and 3, providing 25,300 seats and renewal of the stadium control room, were constructed by Barr Limited within the restrictions of a fully operational football stadium and close to major overhead power lines. Each phase was successfully completed in nine months.

In addition to the standard facilities expected of a modern stadium, the available usable space was maximised in constructing floors for quality offices, hospitality suites, banquet facilities, a leisure club and hotel.

External works involved the regrading of external concourses to provide additional car parking.

Barr Holdings Limited, Heathfield, Ayr, KA8 9SL

High Rise, High Expectations
– lessons to be learned about innovation

IAIN MACLEOD

From several places one can stand back from Glasgow and view it panoramically. A good position, for example, is from the A749 road from East Kilbride into Glasgow. The city centre is not dominated by tall buildings but one sees a large number of high-rise blocks of the order of 20 storeys in the suburbs. As a case study in innovation in the construction industry they provide us with much information for reflection.

In the post-war (1945) years Glasgow had critically difficult housing problems. A large proportion of the population was in sub-standard, unhealthy, slum conditions. Many people lived in tenements with one small toilet cubicle for four families. The city fathers were keen to develop a construction programme which would quickly improve this situation. This was not only a local problem; there was a need throughout the United Kingdom to provide new housing on a grand scale. Some hard thinking was done, a philosophy emerged and a programme was established with the fundamental aim of providing housing quickly, at low cost.

A normal strategy in building design is to try to make each building unique whereas in manufacturing there is a high degree of standardisation. If each motor car had to have a fully customised design then the car would only be affordable by the very rich. But because of standardisation and production line processing, cars are cheap in relation to their complexity. The question was asked – 'Could domestic buildings not be standardised and constructed on a production line basis?'

The answer to this question was the Large Panel Building. These buildings have a structure of storey-height precast-concrete walls and (normally) room-sized floor panels. The concrete was produced under factory conditions which allowed much better control in the casting process than with cast-in-place concrete and greater speed of curing of the concrete. At the site, the panels were hoisted into place using a tower crane and fixed (Figures 1, 2 and 3).

The manufacturing analogy had a good foundation in logic but unfortunately the logic was not subject to sufficient scrutiny. In the manufacturing industry, an initial design is carried out leading to the creation of a prototype which is built, tested and modified. Design errors are ironed out and the system is tuned for optimum performance. If the testing proves satisfactory full scale production follows. In the construction industry, such a development process is not practicable because of the high cost of each product. Improvements in building construction are normally effected on a long cycle based upon performance in use. The mid-century civic authorities were not prepared to wait for testing work to be done. They bought the large panel idea and used it on a major scale.

While not all residents of such buildings are unhappy with their accommodation, these buildings have suffered from a wide range of problems which are now discussed.

SOCIAL ISSUES

Most large panel buildings are high-rise. The concept of 'high-rise' has no precise definition but it tends to be used for buildings which have heights which are greater than their greatest plan dimension, needing passenger lifts of necessity. Typically the large panel buildings in Glasgow have 10 to 25 storeys. People were transferred to these buildings indiscriminately and they proved to be very unsatisfactory for families with young children. Adam McNaughton wrote a famous satirical song about the situation – the *Jeely Piece Song*. The chorus goes:

> Ye cannae fling pieces oot a twenty storey flat,
> Seven hundred hungry weans'll testify to that.
> If it's butter, cheese or jeely, if the breid is plain or pan,
> The odds against it reaching earth are nine-nine tae wan.

Children used to play in the back courts of the tenements of Glasgow under the supervision of mothers who could see them from the back windows. When a child was hungry a mother would throw a 'jeely piece' (bread and jam) down from the upper storey. Mothers who were moved to the tall buildings found that supervision of their children at play was a major problem.

The 'neighbours from hell' problem was also common. Opportunities for disruptive behaviour are increased in high-rise living. The housing authority tried to spread difficult tenants around the community but putting them in high-rise buildings magnified the effects of the bad behaviour. People became reluctant to use lifts which tended to be vandalised.

APPEARANCE

A main reason for not standardising buildings is that variation in form is important in the appearance of urban areas. As built, the large panel buildings had a uniform, unappealing style. Tall buildings can enhance a city by giving it focus and drama. They can have a 'sense of place'. The experience of walking the main streets of downtown New York or of Chicago can be positive. But large panel buildings tend to invoke negative feelings of 'grey' and 'barren'.

STRUCTURAL ISSUES

Some of the large panel systems used in the UK were imported, particularly from Scandinavian countries, and were modified to suit local conditions. Structural designers work to codes of practice and during the development of large panel construction in the 1960s the main code for the design of structural concrete was *CP 114: The Structural Use of Reinforced Concrete in Buildings*.

FIGURE 1
Wall panels
arriving on site.

FIGURE 2
Panel being hoisted.

FIGURE 3
Wall panels
being positioned.

This was originally written for conventional structures and did not address many of the special issues inherent in the design of large panel systems. Some structural engineers recognised this and produced satisfactory designs, but many did not.

In November 1968 there occurred one of the most significant structural failures in recent times. On 16 May a Miss Hodge, who lived on the 18th floor of the 22-storey Ronan Point large panel building in Stepney, London, rose just before 6 am to make a cup of tea. She struck a match to light her gas cooker with the result shown in Figure 4. A gas explosion caused the wall panels at the

FIGURE 4
The Ronan
Point collapse.

FIGURE 5
Good wall-to-floor
connections – the
Tracoba system.

FIGURE 6
Cleat fitted to
provide connection
between floors and
wall.

18th floor level to be blown out. This left the panels above unsupported and they crashed down, the debris loading causing the corner panels below the 18th floor to be torn off. Miss Hodge survived but four people who were in the flats above the 18th floor lost their lives in the collapse. The resulting court of enquiry appeared to be successful in establishing the sequence of events which led to the crash. There was a gas leak which was traced to a faulty nut on Miss Hodge's cooker coupling. That the structure collapsed progressively rather than locally was due to faulty design. A fundamental problem was that the connections between the panels were deemed to be inadequate – with stronger connections the progressive nature of collapse would have been unlikely. Figure 5 shows a large panel system under construction with good structural detailing. It is likely that the Ronan Point collapse would not have occurred if reinforcement of the kind shown in this picture had been specified. The court of enquiry also called into question the wind forces used in the design and criticised some of the fire resistance aspects. A 20-year legal process eventually decided that the main blame for the collapse lay with the structural designers.

As a result of the Ronan Point incident the use of gas in large panel buildings was prohibited and a structural check was made on all large panel buildings in the UK. Many high-rise buildings in Glasgow were found to be structurally inadequate and a programme of repair work was carried out on those buildings which were deemed to be unsafe. In some cases buildings had to be completely evacuated to carry out the work. Figure 6 shows a typical arrangement used in the strengthening work.

Another structural problem emerged in the 1980s. The external walls were constructed using a sandwich of outer and inner leaves of concrete with an internal insulation layer in between. The external concrete leaf was non-load bearing and had to be connected to the inner leaf by ties (Figure 7). With the purpose of creating a high level of durability it was common to specify what was called at the time manganese bronze for the connecting ties. This was not in fact bronze but high tensile brass (an alloy of copper and zinc) with up to 2.5% manganese to increase the tensile strength and hardness. This seemed to be a good specification; is brass not the metal that is used for parts for ships which need special protection against corrosion? Unfortunately high tensile brass is subject to corrosion and stress-corrosion cracking. It proved to be entirely unsuitable for the purpose of the ties. Panels became loose and in some instances fell off, fortunately without injury to persons. A major programme of tie replacement took place in the 1980s using mainly special stainless steel ties fixed from the outside.

CONCRETE DETERIORATION

Concrete is less inert and less durable than is often supposed. The ability of the concrete in large panel buildings to support the building is generally more than adequate but these buildings have suffered from a significant amount of deterioration of the exposed parts of the exterior panels (which are normally non-load bearing). Chloride attack and carbonation have caused deterioration and spalling; stones in the external aggregate and mosaic finishes often tended to come loose. Where a corner of a panel was damaged before fitting it was normally repaired often using inadequate techniques. As a result such corners

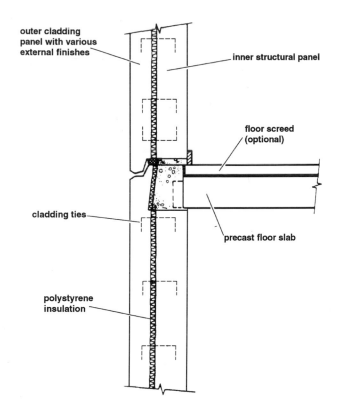

outer cladding panel with various external finishes

inner structural panel

floor screed (optional)

cladding ties

precast floor slab

polystyrene insulation

FIGURE 7
Typical cross-section through external panels showing ties.

became loose, sometimes falling away. Apart from reducing the integrity of the building, bits of concrete falling from a height represent a significant risk to life and limb. The use of overcladding has greatly reduced this risk.

RAIN PENETRATION

Large panel building were constructed all over Europe in the 1960s but those built in Scotland had possibly the greatest need for careful attention to rain penetration. Driving rain will find a way in through the smallest crack. The designers paid special attention to this problem and generally used an 'open-drained joint' approach. The main principle for such joints is that it is difficult to stop high velocity rain so the velocity is reduced before it reaches the main seal. Figure 8 shows a section through an open-drained joint. The force of the rain is dispersed when it passes through the external gap. The water runs down the drain part of the joint. Any water that passes the baffle is stopped by the seal at the back of the joint. But just because you have a good idea in design does not mean that you have got it right. If the seal at the back of the joint is not fitted properly during construction then it cannot be repaired later and in the 1960s sealant technology was much less advanced than it is now. Also there is the potential for water running down the drain to pass through the horizontal joints at the floor levels. The seals at the back of the joints were not normally subject to good quality control procedures and many problems with water penetration have been experienced. This problem has been solved by overcladding (see p112) as can be seen today on many of the tall Glasgow buildings.

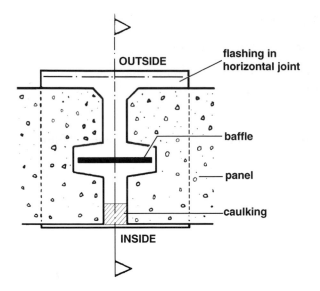

FIGURE 8
Plan section of an open-drained joint.

CONDENSATION

All the walls in large panel buildings are concrete. This provides good soundproofing but a concrete wall has a high thermal mass and if it is cold it acts as a dehumidifier. Many homes are not used during the day and are left unheated. In the evening people come home and have a shower, turn on the kettle and the washing machine. The resulting water vapour condenses on the walls allowing mould to grow causing health problems. The effect is exacerbated by the fact that the houses were 'draught free' to reduce heat loss. But unlike the situation in the past where chimneys for open fires provided good ventilation, modern houses often do not have sufficient air changes. Those who can keep their homes heated have no problems with condensation but poor people often cannot afford to, and do not wish to, maintain comfortable temperatures in all the rooms of their houses. A main motivation for the provision of these buildings was to provide better housing for poor people and it is they who mainly suffer from the problems of condensation. The problems of condensation have been alleviated by providing insulation on the inner faces of the outside walls or behind the overcladding.

OVERCLADDING

Overcladding is the complete covering of the external walls of a building and has had a very significant effect in reducing the problems associated with large panel buildings. If done properly it solves the problem of rain penetration, eliminates the risk of pieces of concrete falling to the ground and helps with the condensation problem. It has also been used to improve the appearance of these blocks by adding colour. However some of the early cladding systems had problems with tearing of the cladding sheets, lack of fire stopping and water penetration. Successful cladding of a high building needs a good understanding of :

- the strength and durability of the materials and how they may interact both structurally and chemically;

- how the fixings work; and

- how the water penetration is controlled.

Some of the cladding systems had to be completely replaced before they were deemed to be satisfactory.

FINANCE

The use of production line methods for large panel buildings did not deliver the cost reductions found in manufacturing industry. Indeed these buildings proved to be more expensive than conventional construction in all cases. Budgets overran and the infrastructure (such as local recreational facilities and community centres) originally planned as part of area developments had to be cut. Thus people were moved from inner city housing areas to new housing areas which could be less desirable than the ones from which they moved.

The Government of the time decided not to provide special subsidies for non-traditional construction in the expectation that competition and the scale of building would eventually result in cheaper housing. This was mistaken; a subsidy in the early stages of development of the numerous systems (there were over 300) would have resulted in much better solutions.

THE VIEW LOOKING BACK

The fundamental motivations for improving the housing stock in Glasgow which prompted the mid-century use of large panel systems were admirable. Poor people were living in sub-standard conditions and something was done quickly to alleviate the problems. But the push to solve these problems in a short time created new conditions which were not necessarily more desirable. It is clear that the drive to get people out of the slums in the shortest practicable time was not the right strategy. The large panel experience showed that it can be dangerous to push ahead with untested innovations on a grand scale. Some of the lessons to be learned are now reviewed.

It can be dangerous to extrapolate from experience in widely different locations. There was much experience of large panel construction in Europe before the main development in the UK. For example, such buildings were successful in cold Eastern bloc countries where heating in the winter is essential and was at that time normally supplied free by the local authority (using combined heat and power schemes for example). But in the west of Scotland the combined effect of rain and frost impose extreme conditions for materials and construction to withstand, probably unique in Europe.

If you are going to develop a structural system on a large scale, guidelines for its design need to be developed. From the structural design aspect, the lack of a code of practice for the design of large panel buildings was a seriously negative factor. Some firms understood the problems of providing good connections and were able to design large panel buildings of great robustness. One example shown at the Ronan Point Enquiry was of a building in Morocco which had a bottom corner room used as an ammunition dump. This was blown up causing only local damage to the building and not causing any progressive collapse (Figure 9). Thus the Ronan Point collapse did not show that the large

FIGURE 9
Large panel
building with only
local damage due
to arms explosion.

panel concept is structurally unsound. It did show that good codes of practice were needed.

During the construction phase of innovative systems there is a need for continuous and expert supervision. The inspections made of large panel buildings after Ronan Point showed that the standard of site supervision was very low in many cases. This is unacceptable in any situation but is particularly remiss when the construction techniques are novel.

When developing a new system or using an existing system in non-standard conditions careful study is needed. Fundamental understanding of how the system works is essential; issues such as how the materials interact, how the parts should be connected, how the building will behave in its environment must be addressed.

It should be noted that not all innovative systems used for housing have been unsatisfactory. For example *no-fines concrete* systems, being of cast *in situ* construction, did not suffer from the problems of rain penetration. In 1974, 25% of all new houses in Scotland were built in no-fines concrete. No major problems have been experienced with this form of construction.

The large panel concept is no longer used in the UK. I believe that the last large panel building to be built in Glasgow was the Thistle Hotel in Cambridge Street and that it has performed successfully. I leave you with the words of Sir Alfred Pugsley, one of the great structural engineers of this century who was a member of the Ronan Point Court of Enquiry. In a tribute to him in the *Structural Engineer* (19 May 1998) following his death at the age of 94, John D. Allen quoted him as saying:

> 'When undertaking the design and construction of a major structure that appears superficially to involve no more than an extrapolation of successful past practice, be wary about treating it in a routine manner. Endeavour rather to instil an atmosphere in the design office, and in the field, appropriate and natural to a non-routine pioneering work, as by the introduction of fresh minds'.

ACKNOWLEDGEMENT

I am grateful to John R. Scott, consulting engineer for reviewing the paper and making very useful suggestions on content.

Armadillo, Glasgow

Climate change is one of the biggest challenges the world faces today. British Steel recognises this and places a great importance in the development of new and improved products and services that make construction easier, more reliable and sustainable. Complete engineered steel intensive solutions can form the backbone to our cities of the 21st century.

British Steel, P.O. Box 1, Brigg Road, Scunthorpe, North Lincolnshire. DN16 1BP

Engineering in the SECC

JIM HAMPSON

The Scottish Exhibition and Conference Centre is adjacent to the River Clyde. The building (Figure 1), christened The Armadillo by the press, dominates the skyline.

The clients for the Scottish Exhibition and Conference Centre researched the needs of potential conference users and it was decided that the auditorium should be capable of providing seating for 3,000 people. This capacity meant the centre could accommodate international conferences which require associated exhibition space.

The clients appointed a team based upon a brief which set out their initial requirements and separate submissions were invited from architects, engineers and quantity surveyors. Ove Arup & Partners, who had recently been involved in large conference facilities at Edinburgh, Birmingham and Osaka, were selected for the engineering design. Arup's brief was to design all of the engineering elements including foundations, structure and all mechanical and electrical (building services) systems. Arups had also been involved in various landmark buildings throughout the world, including the Sydney Opera House and the Pompidou Centre in Paris. The Arups' team for this project had just completed the Edinburgh International Conference Centre. The challenge of engineering this special project, was made even more exciting by its complex geometry and its location on infilled docks adjacent to the Clyde.

Before contemplating the design of engineering elements for a building of this form and complexity it is necessary to take stock of some of the architectural factors:

- the external form
- the internal form
- the separation of the auditorium from the ancillary circulation spaces
- the structure and linking of the auditoria floors to the foyer space at different levels, and
- 5,000 square metres of column-free space.

Of course the shape had not been determined when the budget and programme were set. These constraints reinforced the need for a value-for-money design and affected all engineering elements.

FIGURE 1
The imposing
'Armadillo'
(courtesy Keith
Hunter Photography).

There were many other engineering considerations:

- the need for air conditioning in the auditorium
- the upgrading of existing exhibition facilities
- the special lighting requirements for different functions
- the clients' demands for the flexible provision of water, power, data and drainage, and
- a fast track programme.

FIGURE 2
Romantics might
associate the roof
with the shape of
ships' hulls – a
tangible association
with the past
(courtesy Keith
Hunter Photography).

It was extremely challenging to be designing engineering elements for an important building in a city with such strong engineering roots. The project was located in an area associated with Scotland's renowned shipbuilding heritage.

Over 30,000 ships were launched on this famous river and this building would attract prosperity back to this part of Glasgow. The steelwork had to be designed to allow the architects and cladding specialists to design a cladding system which could be erected speedily and to make the building envelope thermally efficient and impervious to rain (Figures 2 and 3).

The Armadillo is an important icon for Glasgow and in future years everyone will relate to it as the local inhabitants do with the Opera House in Sydney. The world-famous Australian opera house is in concrete and glass but for Glasgow the concrete is restricted to the internal structural elements leaving a superstructure of steel clad in both glass and aluminium. Over 1800 tonnes of steel support over 10,000 square metres of cladding, suspended floors and balconies. Designing the structure of a building with such complex geometry involved the production of over 4000 drawings detailed in such a way as to allow a very fast rate of steelwork erection. The structure is made more significant and more complex by the incorporation of a flytower. The arches supporting the shells enclose the entire volume of the auditorium and the flytower. The avoidance of columns allows a free and unobstructed view of the stage. The shape of the structure was dictated by both the maximum curvature which allows straight aluminium sheets to be used so avoiding the alternative and extremely expensive use of pre-curved sheeting and also by the creation of a dramatic entrance foyer.

FIGURE 3
During the construction phase with the steelwork 'skeleton' gradually being covered by aluminium sheets (courtesy Keith Hunter Photography).

A radius of 38 metres was selected and all shells were cut from cylinders of this radius.

The load from the structure is resisted by the inclined arched trusses (see Figure 5). This incline results in an overturning force which must be resisted to balance the structure. The two main arched trusses are therefore tied together with cross bracing which provides additional strength.

The thermal movement of the structure is of interest in that the Armadillo behaves like a large accordion with significant movements on the extreme eastern tip above the glazed wall. The movement associated with these thermal effects had to be carefully considered at all stages of the design.

The arches act in bending as well as in compression. The roof steelwork was analysed using specialist software. A computer model containing all elements was constructed to analyse:

- forces in the arches
- thermal effects
- stress checks for all the elements; and
- movement of the shells under snow and wind loading.

The analysis demonstrated how efficient the arches were in binding the Armadillo together to resist wind forces.

The strength of the team in engineering design was complemented by the construction managers, Bovis, and the steelwork fabricators, Watson. Their experience and ingenuity, contributed greatly to the erection of the non-vertical arches (Figure 6).

The major spaces in the building are air conditioned. The intermediate spaces are mechanically or naturally ventilated with space heating. Figure 7 shows the location of one of the air handling plants which serves the main

FIGURE 4
Work in progress on the steelwork (courtesy Bovis Construction).

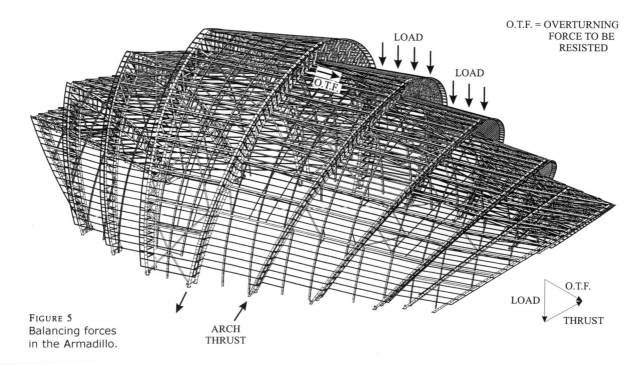

FIGURE 5
Balancing forces in the Armadillo.

O.T.F. = OVERTURNING FORCE TO BE RESISTED

LOAD

LOAD

O.T.F.

ARCH THRUST

LOAD

O.T.F.

THRUST

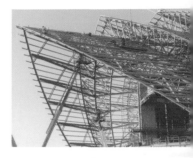

FIGURE 6
(left Section
of the building
illustrating the
orientation of
the arches (courtesy
Watson Steel).

(right) Erection
of the arches.

auditorium. Fresh air is taken into each air handling plant to be heated or cooled, humidified or dehumidified to suit the conditions. From the air handling plant, the treated air is led to a range of ductwork which provides conditioned air to the auditoria. Air is returned from the auditoria by another range of ductwork to the air handling plant for re-treatment. A proportion of this air is exhausted directly from the building to the outside so that an adequate amount of fresh air is continually introduced to the buildings in order to provide a fresh environment.

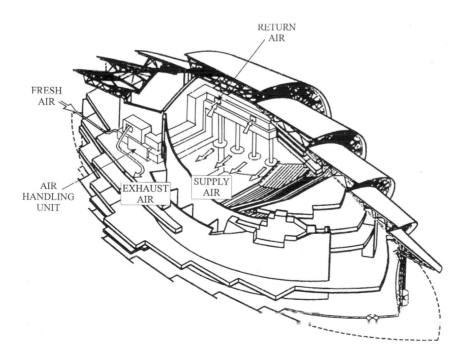

FIGURE 7
Schematic
illustration of the
air handling plant
and patterns of
air flow.

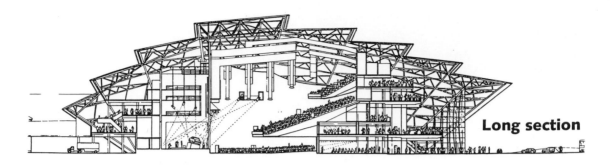

Long section

The main auditorium is flanked on either side by air handling plantrooms at the third floor level. Short routes link the air handling plant with the high level ductwork which serves the auditorium. The shape of the building envelope minimises the space which is available for plant as well as influencing all aspects of the building services design. In order to make the best use of plant space a system of stacked air handling plants with complex air plenums provide distribution routes for air in and out of the building.

It was decided that the ductwork should be exposed within the ceiling space of the auditorium. The combination of large duct sizes (to reduce noise) and the architect's decision to leave an aluminium foil finish creates a dramatic effect (Figure 8).

Less dramatic but equally vital, is the ventilation of the foyer space. A mechanical ventilation system provides heating and ventilation under normal circumstances to cater for an area that will occasionally be very densely populated. A system of automatically operated louvres between the shells open in response to rising internal temperature. This is an effective, economical and unobtrusive approach to an intermittent problem.

The SECC complex is founded in an area that was previously occupied by the Queen's Dock. Whereas the original SECC halls were built on essentially granular fill, rendered suitable for construction using dynamic compaction, a more robust solution had to be found for the conference centre because of its size and weight. The solution involved carrying the structural loads through the dock infill to the bedrock using large-diameter bored piles. The conference centre straddles old quay walls and their positions were established by site investigations. Another complication was that the dock had previously been infilled with demolition rubble fill. The pile locations were chosen to suit the site conditions. teamwork provided close collaboration between the geologists, geotechnical engineers and the structural engineers during the design of the foundations.

FIGURE 9
Internal view of the roof space illustrating the dramatic combination of structural elements and roofing (courtesy Keith Hunter Photography).

ELECTRICAL INSTALLATIONS

The design involved the integration of two megawatts of new electrical load into an existing high voltage network without disrupting the electricity supplies to existing exhibition facilities during construction. Cable containment systems were designed to allow the client space for future additional services and temporary wiring for special functions.

The conference centre is served by an 11kV electrical supply which is stepped down via transformers. From the transformers, low voltage power serves the main switchboard and a secondary essential (emergency) electricity supply is fed direct from a standby generator. Sub-distribution boards throughout the building supply lighting and power requirements.

The building's profile meant that distribution space had to be carefully planned and considerable coordination was needed to route all the cable trunking and trays. Lighting was another challenge. The Clyde auditorium had no fixed ceiling so the house lighting had to be suspended approximately 30 metres up in the air. Aluminium lighting trusses were suspended from the roof steelwork, motorised and synchronised to allow lowering and raising of the houselights for maintenance and lamp replacement. The end result gave a theatrical-type suspension with a lighting level of 400 lux provided for the 3200 seats, complete with full dimming facilities.

The front entrance foyer and circulation spaces were of equal importance and the challenge was not only to highlight the steelwork but create moods: shadowing of lighting around the public walkways. This was achieved by mounting directional floodlights on the buffer wall, directed outwards and reflected back from the shells' inner surfaces.

The Clyde auditorium's vast volume (Figure 10) made demands on fire detection solved by installing seven beam transmitters and receivers. The transmitters were mounted on the lighting bridges to permit easy maintenance. The fire alarm system is integrated with the stage smoke curtain, smoke extract fans, fire doors and full voice evacuation system, interlinked with the existing six exhibition halls away from the conference centre. The security systems are monitored and controlled from the original security office

FIGURE 10
The 3200 seat auditorium on three levels (courtesy Keith Hunter Photography).

about 200 metres from the new conference centre. A network of containment and outstations allowed the CCTV and intruder alarm systems to function remotely.

Together with the normal elements of electrical design, production lighting and sound, video, signage, data and telecommunications had to be provided.

The building form utilises the glazed entrance and the slots between the shells to allow daylight to enter and artificial light to be emitted (Figure 11). The Armadillo is a testimony to the skills of many engineers and craftsmen and a reflection of the enterprise and foresight that has always been apparent in the city.

The team

Consulting engineers for civil, structural and building engineering services	*Ove Arup & Partners Scotland*
Quantity surveyors	*Gardiner & Theobald*
Architect	*Sir Norman Foster & Partners*
Management contractor	*Bovis Construction (Scotland) Limited*
Client's representative	*TTPM*

FIGURE 11 The impressive entrance foyer at dusk which easily creates a number of evocative images.

1880s

1980s

Transformation of Queen's Dock to the Scottish Exhibition & Conference Centre

With increasing pressure on space within urban areas, the need to redevelop redundant sites is well established. Throughout the UK former dockland sites have become prime targets for regeneration projects and Glasgow is no exception in this respect.

The pictures above portray the development history of Queen's Dock from its construction in the 1880s to its infilling in the 1980s to its current use as the home of the Scottish Exhibition and Conference Centre.

Page sponsored by the *URS Corporation* divisions located in Glasgow.
Thorburn Colquhoun – civil, structural and transportation engineers.
Dames & Moore – environmental, programme and construction management.

The Broomielaw, Atlantic Quay

LAWSON CLARK

INTRODUCTION

Atlantic Quay, Broomielaw is formally established as a major city-centre waterfront location. Phase 1 of this unique project totals 280,000 sq ft of high-quality office accommodation and has attracted major companies such as Stakis Plc, Bae SEMA, TSB Bank plc, UAP Insurance, British Telecom and Scottish Power plc.

The developers, Pillar Property plc and Bellhouse Joseph Ltd are now promoting Phase 2, The Broomielaw, which combines high-quality offices with hotel, leisure and other related uses at Atlantic Square, together with three further sites for high-quality office use. Phase 2 includes the South West Regional Headquarters for British Telecom.

The Atlantic Quay development has regenerated an area of Glasgow which had become a decayed and derelict blot on the city's landscape after a period of activity from the early 19th through to the early 20th century.

The Broomielaw was established around the 17th century as Glasgow's port, and developed rapidly from humble beginnings. In the early 1800s it could be compared with a modern day distribution complex, with river-front transit sheds which dispatched and retrieved cargo to and from ocean-going vessels. Adjacent storage was provided in large warehouses and imported cargo, including tea and tobacco, was distributed to all parts of the United Kingdom.

Warehouses were also erected to store home produce, including grain and whisky, which were transferred to the transit sheds and thereafter loaded on ships for export. A notable warehouse, the façade of which remains, is The Queens Tea Store. The warehouse buildings constructed on the site maintained the city grid but, due to their magnitude, demanded a greater footprint than the normal city blocks. The smaller city grids are evident north of Broomielaw and beyond Argyle Street, where they eventually conform to a domestic scale. Bellhouse and Joseph recognised the significance of the large city blocks at Broomielaw and had the vision to capitalise on the potential of creating floor plates with large footprints similar to those being developed in Broadgate, London.

The possibility of attracting large institutions was realised. It was also recognised that the city centre of Glasgow was enclosed by the River Clyde, the Kingston Bridge, the M8 and the new merchant city development to the west, north and east respectively. It was considered inevitable that the expanding city would progress toward The Broomielaw. From an early stage the idea of redeveloping the site was encouraged by the City Council and Scottish Enterprise. In 1985 The Broomielaw was just a wasteland of deserted, crumbling warehouses, a gloomy relic of its past and the opportunity to revitalise a major area of dereliction was fully supported by all who had an interest in the future of Glasgow.

Initial proposals were prepared which matured into a long-term commitment to the site and its surroundings.

HISTORY

Early plans indicate the area remained undeveloped until around the early or middle part of the 18th century. A map prepared by James Barry and dated 1775 shows the first development in the west and recorded the presence of a road identified as 'Broomylaw' on the north bank of the River Clyde.

A plan of 1778 indicates the presence of a small complex of buildings which were identified as 'Delphfield' and contained two large circular structures. Records indicate this was the 'Delphfield' Pottery, an important element of the Scottish ceramic industry during the late 18th and early 19th centuries.

Between 1778 and 1797 the Broomielaw area underwent much residential and commercial building. By 1808 numerous industrial and warehouse buildings had been erected and development of the Broomielaw area followed the typical layout of the city grid. In 1839 the area comprised densely-packed buildings, many of which remained until the late 1980s. The area generally has a history of use for commerce and warehousing and from the late 19th century a number of industries, such as

printing	late 19th century
preservative manufacture	early – mid 20th century
rubber and asbestos manufacture	early 20th century
haulage contracting	early 20th century
printing	mid 20th century

FIGURE 1
An early engraving illustrates the busy nature of the waterfront in the area of the Broomielaw.

In addition, paper stainers, tinsmiths and the manufacture of lead pipe, asbestos and insecticide has occurred in this area, primarily between 15 and 21 York Street.

GENERAL GEOLOGY AND GROUND CONTAMINATION

The superficial geology comprises made ground (i.e. raised by fill) arising from reclamation of the site. These deposits are up to 3.5 metres thick and overlie river alluvium comprising sands, silts, and clays with occasional sand, gravel and cobble deposits.

The underlying rocks consist of sandstones, siltstones and mudstones with occasional limestone bands and thin coal seams representative of the upper limestone group of the Carboniferous system. The strata dip towards the south-east at about eight degrees.

The site investigation identified some low levels of contamination which had to be accounted for in the design of the development. The contamination was removed with the made ground during the construction of basements for the new developments and the excavated materials were acceptable for disposal at a local landfill site.

Extensive tests were undertaken during the site investigation to establish the levels of groundwater and the whereabouts of perched water, i.e. water at a higher than normal level because of underlying impermeable strata. These are always important aspects of new developments.

Raised sulphate concentrations were also recorded and the protection of buried concrete from sulphate attack was therefore required in the design.

Water sources which could have been affected by the migration of contaminants included groundwater and the adjacent River Clyde. Evidence from the historical review and site investigation indicated the level of contamination in the groundwater was unlikely to impact significantly on these sources, particularly when recognition was given to the dilution potential of the river.

Site neighbours were also unlikely to be affected by the migration of contaminants unless methane and carbon dioxide were found to be present within the site. Subsequent monitoring confirmed that methane gas was not present and that the concentration of carbon dioxide was well within accepted limits.

ARCHAEOLOGICAL INVESTIGATION

Historical records indicated archaeological remains associated with the former Delphfield Pottery could have existed within the site boundaries. However, given that previous demolition works included the removal of basements and buried foundations, it was considered unlikely that any significant archaeological remains would be found. Subsequent investigations confirmed this to be the case.

REGENERATION

Atlantic Quay is a prestigious city centre site close to the main road and air links and the architecture endorses the high profile of the site. There is no compromise in the choice of materials with the visual impact of a glass and steel-ribbed colonnade curving around the south-east development (Figure 2). The pink granite, for example, complements the old tradition of red sandstone in the city.

As part of the initial phase, residential flats were constructed around a courtyard and behind a listed façade in James Watt Street. The construction of a piles foundation in close proximity to existing structures required care to minimise the effects of ground disturbance, noise and vibration and a non-displacement pile type was adopted.

THE BUILDINGS

The new commercial development on the Broomielaw commenced in the late 1980s and has progressed continuously. It currently comprises four new office buildings totalling approximately 500,000 sq ft located between Robertson Street and James Watt Street.

The first three structures, constructed between 1989–1992, consisted of eight and nine-storey structures. The buildings have basement car parking linked by a main entrance ramp from Robertson Street to an underground common turning area. In order to maintain continuity in the construction process the structural form of each building remained similar.

The permanent basement construction consists of reinforced concrete slabs and walls. Due to a high perched water table at the north of the site, the basement was designed as a water-resistant structure with external waterproof membrane and waterbars (usually a built-in plastic jointing strip which excludes water after the concrete has hardened).

The superstructure consists of a structural steel frame, with a typical column grid of 8.l metres x 8.l metres which provided relatively large open areas within each of the floors and at the same time accommodated parking requirements within the basements. The structural floors use composite construction made up of concrete slabs and profiled metal decking and shear studs (steel welded to say a rolled-steel joist to ensure composite action of the steelwork and concrete slab). The lateral stability for the buildings is provided by the floor and vertical diagonal steel bracing located in the stair cores.

FIGURE 2
The new Broomielaw development standing boldly among the more traditional architecture of Glasgow.

The fourth building located between York Street and James Watt Street is a seven-storey office, completed in 1998 and forms the South West Regional Headquarters for British Telecom. Once again the proximity of adjacent existing buildings necessitated the use of particular methods for the foundations, to minimise disturbance. At the north-east side of the building there remained the existing stone façade, The Queens Tea Stores, which required underpinning during the construction of the main underground service vehicle turning area.

The superstructure in this building consists of a steelwork frame with a typical structural grid of 15 metres x 7.5 metres with secondary steel beams placed at 3-metre centres. Mechanical and electrical service distribution routes pass through pre-formed holes in the web of the beams. The floors again are of composite construction and the steel vertical bracing is located within the stair and core walls.

The granite wall cladding (i.e. the outer skin which does not carry any load) on the first three buildings consists of a cavity wall construction with two leaves of 100 mm dense blockwork and an outer granite facing. The walls are supported at each floor level and soft joints were located at the head of the panels to allow for differential movement between the structural frame and the masonry. The glazed cladding of the fourth building consists of aluminium-framed curtain walling systems (that is glass held in a frame) with mullions spanning vertically. The cladding is supported both vertically and horizontally at each floor on custom-made galvanised steel brackets which are fixed to the slab.

When completed the nine-acre site will provide approximately one million square feet of high quality accommodation. The site is planned to satisfy the most sophisticated space requirements within a family of buildings. In addition, a range of environmental improvements will be undertaken in partnership with Glasgow Development Agency and Glasgow City Council. These relate specifically to visual environmental improvements around Atlantic Quay and to the entrances to Central Station as well as improving pedestrian safety by widening footpaths.

AWARDS RECEIVED

A number of awards have recognised the excellence of this development in diverse ways. These include:

- Scottish Enterprise
  The Royal Incorporation of Architects in Scotland
  Regeneration Design Award 1991
  Commended in Category New Buildings

- Glasgow Award Scheme celebrating the 25th anniversary of The Scottish Civic Trust Diploma of Excellence for outstanding work to improve the physical environment within the City of Glasgow

- The Incorporation of Gardeners of Glasgow Commendation for the year 1992

- Stone Design Awards 1993. Special Award – New Buildings.

The Buchanan Galleries

Another impressive Glasgow landmark that was completed during 1999.
Bovis Scotland handed over the Buchanan Galleries to the developer,
Buchanan Partnership, a joint venture between Slough Estates PLC and
Henderson Investors, an AMP company.

The Buchanan Galleries, which cost £85 million to build, comprises some
600,000 square feet of retail space, 300,000 of which is taken up by anchor
store John Lewis. A further 75 stores, including Sainsburys, Habitat, Next
and Boots, together with a food court and crêche, occupy the remaining
space over two principal levels. A further 600,000 square feet is occupied by
Scotland's largest city centre car park, with parking for over 2000 vehicles.

Bovis Construction (Scotland) Limited, Station House, 34 St. Enoch Square,
Glasgow, G1 4DH

Kvaerner – Govan Shipyard
– a different approach

ROBERT WILSON

SUMMARY

In 1989 the Fairfield shipyard on the River Clyde in Glasgow became the Kvaerner-Govan shipyard and started a new lease of life under Norwegian management. Parts of the works were retained but a significant area of the yard was demolished to make way for the new 'tank shop', and Berth Number One was adapted to a new way of assembling the hull of a ship. The description that follows includes a short account of the new method of assembly, and engineering anecdotes that illustrate some of the significant developments that were used to refurbish the yard.

THE NEW APPROACH TO SHIPBUILDING

In order that the scale of the changes can be appreciated it is necessary to describe the not inconsiderable feats of engineering that were achieved before.

A steel ship is assembled from a multitude of shaped assemblies, some as big as the front of a three-storey house. The load that can be lifted by a crane sets the limit, and the Clyde shipyards were noted for their skyline with the large (for their day) 200-ton capacity tower-cranes. One of these, no longer in use, has been preserved and is a landmark near Bell's Bridge. Another is still in use within the Kvaerner-Govan shipyard.

FIGURE 1
Kvaerner Govan
200-ton capacity
crane.

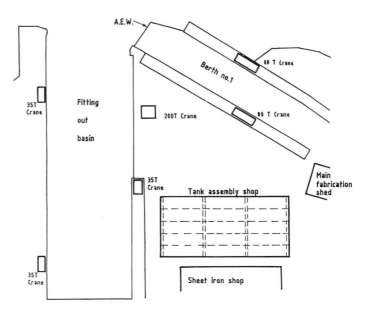

A.E.W.

Berth no.1

00 T Crane

00 T Crane

35T Crane

Fitting

out

basin

200T Crane

Main fabrication shed

35T Crane

Tank assembly shop

35T Crane

Sheet iron shop

FIGURE 2
General arrange-
ment showing the
Tank shop and
Berth No1. The
River Clyde is to
the top of the
diagram.

Most of the assemblies are built up, using welding, from steel plates. These arrive on lorries from the rolling mills in a variety of shapes and thicknesses, because every effort is made to save waste and scrap. The deliveries are made to a schedule that supplies the right plate for the work to be done the next day. The quantities of steel are so large that if delivered all at once, and stacked up, they would fill a football stadium and finding any particular plate would be an impossible task. Each plate has its own identity code and can be called into the fabrication shop when wanted.

The deliveries need to be organised so that the lorries arrive in a convenient sequence and waiting time is minimised. Unfortunately, the schedule can go wrong because of unfavourable weather, breakdowns and accidents and because other people do not always appreciate the logistical problems. From time to time the roads into the yard can become choked with articulated lorries all waiting to unload, and life becomes very difficult.

The steel plates are recovered from the steel plate stockyard, itself about the size of a football pitch, by a gantry crane running on rails. Each plate is marked out on the template floor, another large area. Since many of the finished shapes of the plates are curved or bulbous, the setting out of the flat plates requires the application of geometry. The accuracy required is awesome; a finished assembly is usually required to be set up beside the adjacent assembly on the hull with only ⅛" gap (3 mm) so that the welding of the two plates can be done. In the 'old' days the setting out of the plates was done with steel tapes and Dumpy levels. Frequently, the shape was marked out in chalk on the template loft floor and a full-sized plywood replica constructed. Today this accurate work is done with modern electronic surveying equipment and computer-guided laser-cutting machines.

The shaped plate is transferred to the press shop where heavy machines press the flat plates into the required shapes; for example, the curved edge-plates found under the ship. When the shape is too large for the presses, the curved shape is built up rather like the tail of a lobster. Not all the plates need to be curved. Curves can be built up over a framework, in the manner of a clinker-built dinghy, only very much larger in the shipyard.

Next, the shaped plates are taken through into the fabrication shop. This is a very large roofed hallway. Gantry cranes run on high-level rails along the sides. The dark atmosphere used to be full of fumes from the welding, striped with beams of sunlight and a flutter of flashes, like photographers around a celebrity at night, showing where the welding was being done. The air was full of noise; hammering, hissing, banging, rasping (the abrasive tools cutting or grinding) and of course the voices of the workers trying to make themselves heard above the din. As there were many assemblies being built at once the whole place seemed to be jigging about with movement.

Much of the welding is still done by hand, though the longer runs are done with semi-automatic welding machines. The assembly is often supported off the ground on temporary legs and tack-welded into shape. The space under the assembly allows a transporter to drive underneath and lift the unit. The operators set up the welding machine at one end of the new seam, and the machine travels along the seam, welding as it goes. To protect the liquid weld from the air (the hot metal would oxidise in air, forming rust) a trail of powdered flux is laid and the electric welding arc is submerged beneath it. It can be seen that the process is done 'downhand'. In order that the weld on the other side can be done in a similar manner the whole assembly needs to be turned over.

Each weld may have to be built up with several runs of weld metal in order to control distortion, prevent cracking and allow inspection for flaws. While the piece is being fabricated it may need to be stiffened with ribs so that it can be turned safely. The ribs may be put on before turning, and removed again after turning to allow the welding machine a free run along the seam. The whole process of fabrication is very involved and must, of course, produce a piece of the hull that is fit for its purpose and completely sound.

During turning and later, when being fitted to the hull, the assembly is transported on special vehicles. These transporters are amazing machines, resembling a huge dining table on wheels. The driver sits in a tiny cab hung under one end of the machine and it looks as though the load will squash him. The tabletop can be raised and lowered so that the vehicle can be driven under the load, raised to pick up the load and the load driven away. Although the vehicle can be driven along a road like any other lorry (but not as fast) it can also turn the plane of its wheels through 360°. This means that, for example, the load can be brought alongside and then driven at right angles into place. Imagine parking in a busy street; you drive up beside the opening, turn the wheels through 90° and roll neatly into the parking place!

The transporter has other tricks up its sleeve – the tabletop can be kept horizontal, with the load upon it, even when driving up a ramp or over an uneven surface. As a result, quite tall assemblies can be safely loaded and transported anywhere in the yard – you do not need an expensive level roadway.

Finally, when the assembly has been finished and the welds tested, it can be hoisted and fitted to the hull, adding another 200 tons to the ship. Traditionally, the hull was built out in the open next to the River Clyde. The

FIGURE 3
Berth No1 – the
last hull built in the
traditional way.

berth, a very large U-shaped wedge, was angled to the run of the river to give
the longest reach when the boat was launched. The Clyde is tidal at this part of
the river and the concrete floor of the berth slopes down and finishes at the
very lowest water level. For part of the length the sides are supported by
concrete retaining walls. These are replaced by timber jetty structures beyond.
Along each side there are rail-mounted cranes, but they are smaller than the
200-ton Samson version.

In the traditional manner all ships were built on a timber structure, or
cradle, upon which the keel plates were laid. Gradually the whole length of the
ship was built up, across the bottom (a wide flat area with tapered ends), up the
sides and round the bow and stern, and finally the decks and deck house. The
bulkheads cross the hull from side to side, restraining the sides from bulging
out and dividing the ship's length into compartments; the engine room, the
holds and other areas. The whole ship stood on the cradle structure until it was
ready to be launched, the launch being the first time that any part of the ship
moved. The workers operated outside in all weathers, especially in the early

FIGURE 4
Starting a launch.

FIGURE 5
The characteristic bulbous bow of a modern tanker. The bow thrusters are inside the hole.

days of the building. Later, scaffolds were erected or hung over the sides, and most of the painting was done from these scaffolds.

The procedures were carried over from the days when the plates were riveted together. When welding took over as the method of joining the plates, problems arose and many of the welds had faults in them, which had to be found (using non-destructive testing techniques), cut out and rewelded. Imagine sewing a garment and having to unpick nearly every seam and sew it again! The problems with the welds were creating real trouble because of the delay to delivery and over-run of costs. Morale was also affected because the faults in the welds were not simply bad workmanship, rather that the quality requirements were nearly impossible in the exposed conditions on the berth. When special steels were used because of the very low temperatures needed for the liquid-gas tankers the problems became unbearable. It was time to take a different approach.

A DIFFERENT APPROACH

For some time the smaller ships had been built under cover in large-span buildings. Large doors allowed the finished boat to be launched. The nearby Yarrow shipyard at Whiteinch, Glasgow, produced the navy frigates this way. However, the size of building required to assemble a modern tanker and to have a reasonable expectation of being able to house the super-tankers of the future would be colossal – too big to contemplate even assuming planning permission could be obtained. That was not the way forward.

Developments in Norway, America and elsewhere had made it possible to 'skid' very heavy loads. Skidding is the process of sliding a load using jacks. The jacks are attached to rails; extending the jack will move the load, retracting the ram draws the jack up to a new position ready for the next push on the load. The heavy loads can be sections of the hull. The hull of a tanker is naturally divided into individual storage tanks, at least four, which are assembled end-on to each other. The engine room and bow section are fitted at the respective ends of the ship to complete it.

FIGURE 6
Elevation of the
Tank Assembly
Shop.

35m

35m

136m

64m

Service
entry
door

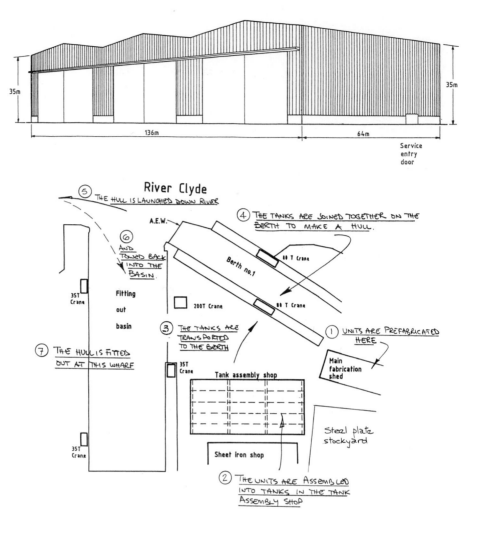

River Clyde

(5) THE HULL IS LAUNCHED DOWN RIVER

A.E.W.

(4) THE TANKS ARE JOINED TOGETHER ON THE BERTH TO MAKE A HULL.

(6) AND TOWED BACK INTO THE BASIN.

Berth no.1

80 T Crane

3ST Crane

Fitting out basin

200T Crane

80 T Crane

(3) THE TANKS ARE TRANSPORTED TO THE BERTH

(1) UNITS ARE PREFABRICATED HERE

(7) THE HULL IS FITTED OUT AT THIS WHARF

3ST Crane

Tank assembly shop

Main fabrication shed

Steel plate stockyard

3ST Crane

Sheet iron shop

(2) THE UNITS ARE ASSEMBLED INTO TANKS IN THE TANK ASSEMBLY SHOP

FIGURE 7
Modern construction
sequence 1 to 7.

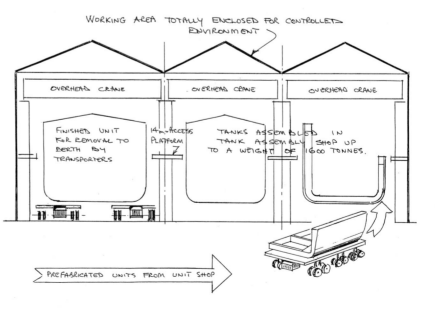

WORKING AREA TOTALLY ENCLOSED FOR CONTROLLED ENVIRONMENT

OVERHEAD CRANE

OVERHEAD CRANE

OVERHEAD CRANE

FINISHED UNIT FOR REMOVAL TO BERTH BY TRANSPORTERS

14m ACCESS PLATFORM

TANKS ASSEMBLED IN TANK ASSEMBLY SHOP UP TO A WEIGHT OF 1600 TONNES.

PREFABRICATED UNITS FROM UNIT SHOP

FIGURE 8
Tanks (parts
of the hull) are
assembled in
the Tank Shop.

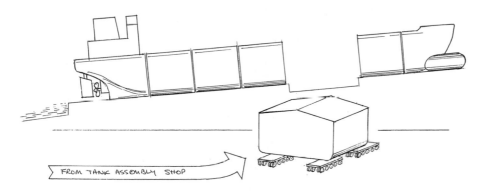

FROM TANK ASSEMBLY SHOP

FIGURE 9
Tank assembly
on the berth.

The sections or tanks could be assembled inside a large building, brought out in sequence and assembled into a complete hull on the slipway (or berth). The shipyard had a large area of old buildings that could be cleared to make way for a new tank shop. The yard could be modified and berth number one converted to the new skidding system. Bigger and better transporters could be bought that would carry the large tanks from the tank shop to the berth. Estimates indicated that completion periods could be halved or even better.

The different approach would involve assemblies from the fabrication shop being delivered to the tank shop where the sections of hull and the deckhouse would be built up under cover and out of the weather in almost ideal controlled conditions. Once built, the tanks of up to 1600 tons would be transported out across the courtyard between the tank shop and the berth and up onto the berth where they could be skidded into position. The sequence would be:

1. Aft end with engine room, rudder and stern thrusters,
2. stern storage tank,
3. middle tank no. 1.

These sections would be joined and slid down the berth. At the appropriate time the deck house would be brought out, lifted above the deck level and the aft end, half of the ship slid up under it, whereupon the deck house could be lowered and secured to the deck.

Part of the reason for starting at the aft end is that the heavy engine would need to be lifted by the 200-ton crane, and in addition there has to be a great deal of fitting and work done inside the hull. It is expected that most of these fittings will be complete by the time the ship is launched. Continuing the sequence:

4. Bow section with bow thrusters,
5. forward storage tank,
6. middle tank no. 2.

These sections are joined together and slid up the berth. Because of the length of the ship and the slope of the berth these sections are above ground. A temporary sloping steelwork structure is erected to carry this half of the ship.

7. Finally the two halves of the ship are slid together and joined. The ship is launched and towed to the nearby fitting-out berth for finishing.

THE NEW WORKS

Early in 1990 preparations for the new tank shop started with the demolition of a range of old buildings on parts of the site. Included were the boiler house, canteen, maintenance and electrical workshops and the air-compressor building. Before these could be taken down all the services had to be re-routed so that the shipyard could continue to function. Many of the more modern services such as the high-pressure water supply, industrial gas supplies and electricity had their positions recorded on drawings and were relatively easy to find. There were the usual problems of manhole covers that would not lift or were lost under stored materials. In a few places the cover had been broken and replaced with a piece of steel plate. Shipyard workers are very inventive! However, the layouts of the older services, such as the drains, were long gone. The incumbent foreman plumber and his retired predecessor were undaunted; putting their combined memories together they were able to identify nearly all the systems, the few bits missing often turned out to be unused pipes. These men must have had to find out all this detail for themselves and develop a corporate memory which was passed on from master craftsman to apprentice, father to son. It is sad to think that modern society does not value this sort of experience.

Service runs that would be in the way of the new works were diverted and the opportunity was taken to rationalise the system. One important sewer ran straight through the middle of the proposed tank shop. The diversion created a potential crisis as for a short time the men were asked not to use the toilets.

Preparation of the site commenced with excavation. Although it had been known that the site had been in continuous use for over a century, much of the buried concrete that was unearthed was unexpected. Certain areas had to be cleared for the piling that would support the main building frame. As the clearance proceeded the site was left looking rather like a first-world-war battlefield, all pitted and uneven.

FIGURE 10
Early days in the
Tank Assembly
Shop area.

It had been decided that the new workshop slab would rest directly on the ground. With the subsoil all pitted and uneven the sought-for uniform bearing pressure (a vital aspect of the design) could not be relied upon, even if the holes were filled up. The variable thickness would allow differential settlements between adjacent areas. It was decided to strip the whole area down to the underside of the old foundations.

To appreciate the magnitude of the task, the plan area of the new workshop was 136 metres long and 64 metres wide. An extra 10 metres was necessary all round for the sloping sides of the hole. Again imagine a football field: all the area inside the front rows of seats would be dug out to a depth of about the height of a room, approximately 3 metres deep.

As the excavations moved westwards the soil changed from clay to sand with extensive pockets of silt and soft clay. The silt had the curious property of appearing to be firm, but if one stood on it and did a sort of rumba with one's feet you quickly sank into the ground! Imagine what would have happened to any building standing on such a soil. All the silt was dug out completely and replaced with some of the granular material from sounder parts of the site.

The waste materials were carted through the shipyard to 'the cowp'; a strange, bare part of the site fringed with willow trees. For years any waste, especially builders' rubble, had been tipped there, spread out a little and left. I recovered a very nice cast-iron screw-down letterpress from the cowp, and my daughter still uses it for her artwork. During the war the cowp was used more positively, having additional slipways built on it for building submarines. Of course it did not have 30 or 40 years of rubble on it at that time. Perhaps, in the future, industrial archaeologists will be delighted to dig it over, and some of the choicest pieces of rubbish will be reverently placed in a museum.

However, the cowp was very useful at the time and took all the surplus soil from the excavations. Care was taken not to spread the soil too high or near the river; we did not want a landslide into the Clyde. Later in the contract the steel frameworks for the doors were assembled there.

Buried in the excavations were several brickwork tunnels. These too needed to be grubbed (cleared) out as well as the mass concrete bases for the compressors. The chimney base, built in reinforced concrete, was broken up over a weekend using a machine that had a passing resemblance to the dinosaur called *Tyrannosaurus rex*. Returning to the tunnels, we were told that the largest tunnel had been a haulway to the long-gone sawmill. Apparently, logs were brought up the Clyde and hauled up this tunnel into the sawmill by horses.

As the tunnel passed under the main roadway and was a potential weakness, it was decided to fill it, and foamed concrete was chosen. Foamed concrete is one of several important innovations in the field of concrete. Made in either of two ways, by mixing a standard concrete with synthetic foam or by using large doses of air-entraining admixture (a compound that enables tiny air bubbles to be held in the concrete mix), the concrete can be made to run like water and rise like bread. These properties allow holes and service trenches to be backfilled safely by pouring the fresh mix straight into the hole from the delivery truck. In this case it was considered dangerous to enter or work inside the old brick tunnel. A bulkhead of plywood was put up and the concrete

FIGURE 11
Silt layer.

FIGURE 12a (left)
The old brick tunnel
to the Clyde.

FIGURE 12b (right)
Inside the old
tunnel.

poured in at one end. When the concrete had hardened the plywood bulkhead was removed.

Before piling could start a platform was formed with the fill material necessary to raise the formation back to the specified level. In fact the contractor raised the platform to the level specified for the topside of the ground slab, and this surface was used as the construction platform for all the works up to the time that the ground slabs were to be constructed. The top layer became contaminated with mud and was stripped off, and the resulting surface was compacted before laying the oversite concrete.

The stone used was an amygdaloidal basalt with some weathered stone. Basalt is a fine-grained igneous rock found as lava flows. It is often quarried and crushed for roadstone. Amygdaloidal refers to almond-shaped inclusions of secondary minerals formed in the gas bubbles. The weathered stone threatened to be a problem as it turned muddy when wetted in a shower of rain. The deliveries were watched carefully and unsuitable material sent away off site.

The general geology and a site investigation indicated that thick beds of silt and sand (already found in the excavations) overlay sandstone bedrock. Experience in and around Glasgow shows that the sandstone was once exposed to wind and rain and the surface (now buried) is crossed with shallow valleys all running into what became the Clyde.

The first site investigation was carried out using a lightweight drilling rig and reached a depth of 23 metres before being halted by dense gravel. A second series of drillings made with different drill equipment penetrated the gravel to the sandstone and also recovered five-metre lengths of the sandstone. This technique is used to sample the sandstone and also to be reasonably sure that the drill has not landed on the top of a large, buried boulder. The depth to bedrock varied, being deeper closer to the river channel. The average value was 31 metres which is probably greater than the height of a church tower.

Clusters of piles were to be used to support the steel columns, or stanchions as they are called. The specification called for a precast concrete segmental piling system. Such a system uses short lengths of concrete pile stock that can be conveniently transported to site by lorry. On site, the full pile length can be made by joining the segments together with special joints. The joint uses metal caps at each end of the segment.

FIGURE 13
Piling.

The pile was driven down to the sandstone bedrock using an hydraulic hammer. The first few blows drove the pile rapidly through the silts and sand. When the point reached the gravel the driving slowed down. The driving rate is measured by counting the number of blows required to drive the pile 300 mm (1 ft). Finally, the pile was driven 'to refusal' (i.e. further blows hardly moved the pile) on the sandstone. The benefit of having precast concrete segmental piles is that virtually any length can be made up to suit the depth to the bedrock. When all the piles in a particular area have been driven, the piling rig moves on and the finished piles are cut to the required length.

Where there is sand the piles in a group have to be driven in a pattern from the centre outwards. This is because the hammering shakes the ground and causes the sand to compact. Otherwise, the first piles would go in quite easily and the last ones hardly at all. Another dangerous problem with driven piling as described above is that the existing walls of buildings may be damaged or cracked. Alongside the new works stands the sheet iron shop, where the ducting used in the ship is made. The main frame of this structure is of steel, but the walls are just panels built between the stanchions (called dado walls). Several of these dado walls cracked quite severely after the nearby piling had been done. Similarly, several cracks appeared in the surrounding roads. Anywhere else these cracks would have been a very serious matter and compensation paid to the owners. As it was the shipyard owned the walls and the roads and the damage was repaired as part of the new works contract.

When the time came to demolish the canteen, which was almost new, everybody said this was a shame. The canteen is a sort of haven, a place to relax, warm yourself on cold days and eat. Anyone accustomed to working in an office cannot imagine how nice it is not to eat at the workplace. The average welder will clock-in and go on board at eight in the morning no matter what the weather is like. If the task is below decks you will be out of the weather, but you will soon be in a dark atmosphere full of smells and any fumes not pumped out by the ventilation system. One has to remember that the ship is

FIGURE 14
Cracks in wall.

being put together and hardly any of the designed services are operational. A string of bulbs, like fairy lights, on a safe 110 voltage lights the working space, which may be cramped in between the outer hull and the liquid-gas tank inside. The hull is like a huge drum being beaten by a hundred men; the slag needs to be chipped out of the weld after each pass, and then there is the grinding. Calls of nature have to be answered and time may be short, even though the policy is to provide portable toilets throughout the working area. Who in their right mind would want to open their packet of 'sarnies' in such a place?

So the canteen is a haven and the men want to have their full break-time in it. The old canteen was in the middle of the yard and could be reached in five minutes from almost anywhere. The new canteen was away over the other side of the fitting-out basin and a good 15 minutes from anywhere but the cowp. Teabreaks and mealtimes stretched out to an hour or more and productivity was affected. Fortunately for the site staff the canteen was just behind the site offices, and we were able to pop in for a bacon roll first thing in the morning, about 7.45 am. One morning we went in for our usual snack to find the entire canteen staff filling rolls and making urns of tea! A different approach was under way – the mobile vending van. Now the food came to the men served by the pretty girls from the canteen. The breakfast queues were long and lively.

Lunch, a longer break than breakfast, was still served in the canteen as the men had enough time to walk over there. It was when the new canteen started up that a heart-warming social activity became apparent. Formerly, if one was rather late for lunch, one noticed some groups of old men and women waiting around near the canteen. These transferred themselves to the new canteen when it opened. These old folk were the pensioners and their wives of the old Fairfield Yard and they were invited to come in for a free meal after the general rush. It is nice to think that the commercial scramble did not need to find a different approach to this old custom.

In the days when the yard was being cleared for the new buildings, several trades and crafts had to be relocated. It is not often realised how varied these skills are. Practically everything on board ship is made by the yard, or designed and subcontracted out. In the deckhouse there are cabins, mess rooms and even a small swimming pool. There are kitchens, freezers, store rooms, first-aid room, laundry and drying room, toilets and shower rooms and, of course, the bridge, radio room and related working areas. So there are ventilating systems, miles of wiring, lighting and heating, plumbing and panelling all fitted by the appropriate trades.

As in the services there is a class system, with the professional grades at the top – they eat in the 'Golden Trough' and wear white overalls about the site (never in the dining-room, please!). Then there are the supervisory grades and office staff – they eat in the little dining-room. The supervisory grades wear red overalls so that they can be easily found when needed. Lastly come the general workers who eat in the canteen and wear blue overalls. Language is interesting too – the senior executives speak Norwegian and slightly American English, the supervisory grades have a broader Scottish twang verging into Govan and the general workers can be very broad Govan and almost incomprehensible to a mere English speaker. 'Govan' is a dialect of 'Glasgow' and sets the speaker proudly apart from others.

The purpose of all the work was to construct a three-bay, steel-framed shed in which the tanks could be assembled from the pieces made in the fabrication shop. The dimensions, as has been said before, are large by any standard, rising nearly 40 metres in the air (as tall as a twelve-storey block of flats). Even the doors are huge, 26 metres high and 42 metres wide (in a bay width of 45 metres).

Twin overhead electric cranes serve each bay with a main hook load of 80 tonnes and a secondary hook load of 15 tonnes. The cranes are able to lift and move in tandem, giving a unit load of 160 tonnes (a tonne is the metric equivalent of the old ton). Each bay is able to work independently of the adjacent bays.

The frame has three bays, each having a 45-metre span. The height varies from 37 to 40 metres.

Each tank assembly shop has been designed to accommodate the assembly of 1600-tonne ship sections (equivalent to a parcel of 160 empty double-decker buses). The sections will be completed on the shop floor with the aid of the overhead cranes and then transported to the slipway berth on multi-wheel transporters.

FIGURE 15
Fitting a stanchion onto its holding-down bolts.

FIGURE 16
Doors being erected.

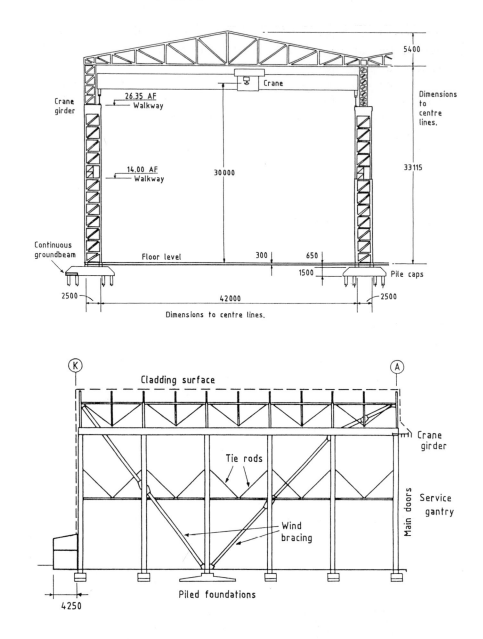

FIGURE 17
Structure cross-
section.

FIGURE 18
Elevation showing
wind bracing.

The whole of the superstructure, including the cranes, is supported on
'heavy' steelwork (heavy as in heavy industry). The principal stanchions are
made up from two I-beams, the largest available, cross-braced in a zigzag
fashion using angle sections to form a kind of tube. (If the stanchion had
been laid on its side it would have been possible to drive a small car along
inside it.) These big sections rose to the 14 metre AF (above floor) walkway
level where they were spliced to similar large sections. The splice was necessary
to allow the sections of stanchion to be transported from the factory, where
they were made, to the site and to limit the weight that had to be lifted by
the erection cranes.

People have asked why it was that at the shipyard, which was accustomed
to working with steel, they did not build their own steel frame. Very simply,

this was because all the resources were fully engaged in finishing the tanker that was on the slipway so that berth number one could be cleared for the renovation works to begin.

The steel stanchion section changes at the 26.35 AF level. It becomes the continuation section that supports the roof and makes enough space for the welded plate girders to be fitted in for their support. The girders support the rails on which the overhead cranes run. The plate girders for the crane rails need to be very stiff and are designed as fully continuous over the 12.8 metre spans between the stanchions. Such a single length cannot be transported or lifted and so the girder was supplied in two lengths and welded together on site. The welding was done inside a small enclosure hung around the joint so that wind and rain did not affect the welding process. Such important welds are inspected and tested non-destructively. The weld may be X-rayed to find any cavities or slag inclusions or swabbed with a penetrant dye that enters small cracks and then shows up under ultraviolet light. Any faults have to be cut out and the weld repeated.

The running rails are fixed to the top flange with clips and have special rubber pads under the rail to absorb vibration. To prevent the crane running off the end of the rail there are special electrical switches that cut off the power and apply brakes. There is also a buffer fitted on the end of the rail.

The roof trusses were fabricated from rectangular hollow sections that were welded into sections for transport to site. On site the trusses were bolted together. Each section had end plates welded onto the ends of the spars. Two sections were laid out flat on the floor of the tank shop and brought together. This meant both alignment and level; old railway sleepers and wedges were used to make low supports and the steelwork was laid on top. The end plates were drawn together with old-fashioned 'turfers'. This is a corruption of the French words *tir fort*, meaning to pull hard. By using podger spanners, which have a long tapering handle that can be slipped through a pair of matching

FIGURE 19
Lifting a roof truss.

holes, the connection can be aligned and the first bolts inserted. It is a basic safety rule in steelwork erection that you keep your hands and fingers out of the connection. A podger can be straightened out if the joint moves unexpectedly, but a finger will be lost if it is severed.

When each truss had been assembled on the floor, two cranes were positioned and the truss was lifted into place by the two cranes working as one. The design has to take account of the fragile nature of the truss when it is on its side. The truss can buckle when it is first lifted. Once it is upright it is safe because this is the attitude that it was designed for. Lifted to the top of a pair of stanchions it is held while workmen fix the truss to the stanchion tops. Before the lifting chains are released a number of rafters are fixed to brace the truss and stop it falling over sideways. The old practice of walking on the steelwork as it was put up has been discontinued. New safety rules require all steelwork to be fixed with the men safely in a special cradle hung from a crane or from a vehicle mounted access platform (VMAP) generally called a 'cherry picker'. Very occasionally men have to get out of these safe platforms onto the steelwork. Before this can happen a risk analysis has to be made and a method of work decided. When everything has been planned a permit to work will be issued and its conditions carefully followed. Safety is now taken very seriously and the old image of the rugged constructor has been banished. All construction sites are hard-hat areas and helmets must be worn. With steelwork erection above you there is little need to remind folks; hammers, spanners and bolts have all been dropped accidentally. In the safety records there are several cases where a man's life has been saved by his helmet.

The use of rectangular hollow sections (RHS) has been mentioned. In the early days steel could only be obtained in solid rolled sections. Today there are a number of additional types including RHS, tubular hollow sections and cold-rolled sections. A rectangular section has several advantages: it is lighter than the solid, it is very stiff and rigid, the inside cannot weather and only the outside needs to be painted. In addition the joints are easier to make than with tubular sections. The use of RHS in the tank shop trusses, coupled with a very rigorous analysis using the benefits of computers, resulted in a very economical design and reduced the total weight of structural steelwork from an estimated 2000 tonnes to 1500 tonnes.

The holding-down (H-D) bolts used to fasten the stanchion to the pilecap are very big; in this case 50 mm (2 inches) diameter and some 3 metres long (10 ft). The group of 8 or 12 H-D bolts were fitted with anchor plates and a top template to ensure that they were in the right place when the stanchion was lowered onto them. The whole assembly weighed a little less than a tonne and in size and weight would be similar to the larger family car.

Survey stations were set up early in the contract. These were located well away from the edges of the site to avoid them being disturbed by the piling. A constant problem was that the shipyard was using all areas surrounding the site. With the help of the project office all parties were informed and this generally avoided obstruction of sight lines or the overplacing of a survey station. Although traditional instruments were used throughout the contract, all critical dimensions were checked using electronic distance measurement (EDM). During the piling works a young couple, husband and wife, visited the

FIGURE 20
Steel framework.

site and set out the next day's work. They were employed as subcontractors, brought their own instruments and equipment and did a very good, efficient job.

The steelwork was erected before casting the workshop floor for a number of reasons:

- the holding-down bolts were below slab level and access to them was easier without the surrounding slab;

- the steelwork was on the 'critical path' of the programme and any delay would have had serious knock-on effects upon the cladding and fitting out of the tank shop, particularly the electric overhead cranes;

- with the slab sub-programme trailing into the back end of the year the protection from the cladding would considerably improve the working conditions.

Each of the six overhead cranes was delivered in one piece, by road. When transporting a 42-metre long box-girder section by road it is necessary to make special traffic arrangements: the deliveries were made very early on selected Saturdays and Sundays. Each main girder was supported at one end on the tractor unit and at the other end on a motorised trolley that could be steered independently. Opposite the main gate of the yard was a leafy park with the usual iron fence along the edge. Before the delivery was made careful measurements were taken of the width of the road and the height of the fence. The first girder arrived at about two o'clock in the morning and the drivers proceeded to manoeuvre it into the yard gate. All activities came to a grinding

FIGURE 21
Lifting-in the
crane girder.

FIGURE 22
Lifting-in the
crane girder.

halt when it was discovered that the girder would not fit over the top of the fence. After some investigation it was discovered that the height of the fence had been measured from the pavement, whereas the trolley actually stood on the road. The road was lower than the pavement by the height of the kerb, some four inches. The fitter literally cut us out of our predicament by cutting down the fence (it was restored later and repainted as an act of goodwill). However, when the park keeper arrived to start his day he found all his fencing on the ground and nearly had a fit! Canteen tea revived him and he saw the funny side of it all.

Once the crane girder was in the yard it was fitted with the running wheels and control cab and the whole unit was lifted in the afternoon as a single lift by a 500-tonne giant mobile crane. This was so big that it needed another crane to help it erect itself. Hung from the middle of the girder the gantry crane was balanced very carefully so that it hung horizontally. Two teams of fitters drew the ends carefully onto the rails. The accuracy was perfect. Each girder was winched back under a section of the roof ready for it to be connected to the electricity that would drive it. Later it would be slowly run up and down the rails to ensure a perfect fit.

As each bay became available, a bulldozer cleared the muddy and contaminated stone working platform, and the surface was levelled and recompacted. The construction was a final layer of selected crushed stone, a topping or icing of 'oversite' concrete to give a clean surface and the structural slab of heavily-reinforced concrete. Within the structural slab were further steel sections, which were connected to form an earthing system. Electric arc welding was used almost exclusively and involves the welding rod being one terminal with the circuit completed by connecting the steel fabrication to the earthing system. The top flange of the earthing steelwork is flush with the top of the concrete slab; the bottom flange is surrounded in concrete.

The concrete used was a designed mix using a Portland cement and ground-granulated slag binder. Modern concrete technology has developed a number of blended binders that replace the traditional cement. Two of these binders use waste material from either the power stations (pulverised fuel ash or pfa) or steel production (slag or ggbs). The properties of the hardened concrete are improved and the use of waste material is environmentally good. Plasticisers and super plasticisers (more admixtures) are particularly useful in modifying the properties of the raw concrete.

Because of the size of the floor bays the concrete was delivered to the doorway and pumped to the point where it was to be placed. The concrete pump was lorry mounted with a long pipe boom that could reach into the building. The end of the pipe was a flexible rubber hose positioned by two men. More men spread the liquid concrete and compacted it. The primary finishing used a Bunyan finisher that was developed in America. A 200 mm diameter (8 inches) steel tube spans the pour and is caused to spin towards the concrete by an independent hydraulic turbine fitted to one end of the tube. The operator controls the spinning while drawing the tube along rails; another operator assists with the movement of the Bunyan at the other end.

The concrete surface is spread slightly higher than the finished level required and the Bunyan driven against it. The concrete is compacted and smoothed as it passes under the quickly spinning tube. The first pass is followed by a second for a smoothing effect. The edges are compacted by immersion vibrators and float-finished by hand with the steel being cleaned of mortar to expose it. The final finish is by power float and power trowelling when the concrete is stiff enough to walk on.

These slabs were cast near the end of the year and the evenings were turning cold. One evening there was the first frost and the finishers, with their power floats, were ready to start work at about eight o'clock in the evening. The rest of us had had a busy day casting that particular slab and were ready to go home.

Normally concrete stiffens enough for it to be walked on in about an hour, two at the most. This night it would not stiffen because of the cold, frosty weather. The finishers were still working on the slab at 10 o'clock next morning; and when they did eventually finish they had to rush off to their daytime job somewhere else. After this the concrete was changed to a Portland cement-without-slag mix which stiffens more quickly.

CONSTRUCTION IN THE BERTH

The River Clyde is tidal at this point, rising three metres at each tide. This brings the water halfway up the slope of the berth. Consideration was given to forming a cofferdam (a temporary dam to exclude water) to keep the water out and allow continuous construction. However, the cofferdam was impractical and it was decided to work between tides. This was not too difficult as the shipyard works round the clock and is consequently well-lit.

In principle the works were straightforward, requiring the construction of four parallel lines of concrete, two launchways and two skidways. These strip foundations extend from the lower end of the ramp, known as 'aft end ways' or AEW, up the slope of the berth, up the artificial slope between retaining walls and onto an elevated portion.

The complication is that the top surfaces follow a closely defined parabolic curve. The reason for this curved surface is because when the ship is launched it must slide slowly to start with. As the aft end (the ship is launched propeller-end first) becomes waterborne the hull tends to span from stern to bow, which puts a very heavy load on the bow supports. In this condition it is necessary to accelerate the launch. The top part of the slipway is nearly flat but becomes progressively steeper as it nears the AEW, thereby causing the ship to speed up at the critical moment.

The launchways will be used many times and are capped with steel plates to resist the wear. Clearly, with the heavy loads there can be no voids under the steel plates and a close contact is required between the concrete and the steel. Eventually, after several alternative approaches were tried, the concrete was cast slightly low and a thin topping was spread over the surface before laying the steel plates. In this way the plate squeezed the surplus fresh mortar out but conformed to line.

During the work on the berth a number of obstructions were found and removed. The first was a timber pile, which proved most obstinate, and the other obstructions were several concrete walls about 1500 mm thick, two steel plates about 40 mm thick, complete with rows of rivet holes at the edges and a whole assortment of pipes and services.

IN CONCLUSION

The application of a different approach to all phases of a construction job can be found in these anecdotes. Colleagues will, no doubt, remind me of others. In design we use computers, allowing us to use more sophisticated methods of analysis and more efficient steel sections. In the planning of a job we can identify the critical activities. In the setting out and other survey work we use 'clever' instruments and can fix our position using satellites. Safe working practices have been introduced and are backed up with safety law. The process of shipbuilding has been revolutionised using techniques of heavy lifting adopted from the offshore oil industry. Large-span structures enable all-weather construction. The list could go on.

LIST OF PARTICIPANTS
The client was Kvaerner-Govan Ltd.
The structural designer was Gronstad & Tveito AS, Bergen, Norway.
The main contractor was Balfour Beatty Construction.
The piling was designed, supplied and installed by Hercules Piling Ltd.
Structural steelwork was fabricated and erected by George Depledge and Co. Ltd.
Structural steelwork for the berth and for the fabrication shop gable end
was supplied, fabricated and erected by Kingdom Engineering Ltd.
Cranes were designed and supplied by Kone Cranes Ltd.

*End note: As of July 1999, the shipyard moved into a new era when GEC Marconi became the new owners. Although the nature of contracts may change, the yard's survival has been confirmed.

An Editorial Perspective

This final chapter was suggested and then written rather late in the development of the book. It became clear when all the chapters had been received that there is another story to tell of the engineering of buildings, that of the individual engineers who have contributed so much to Glasgow. This brief chapter can only mention a few from the many; and then only in selected disciplines. However, it is hoped that those included give a fair indication of the tremendous influence that all Glasgow's engineers have had. It should also be noted that this influence has been international. The editor of the book remembers on several occasions abroad visiting a famous bridge or structure only to find the name of a Glasgow engineer inscribed on the steel or masonry.

Sir William Arrol was one of Glasgow's great engineering characters, if not the most famous. He was energetic and inventive and the riveting machines used on the Forth Bridge were of his own design, and developed to overcome the problems of constructing this major engineering structure. Of humble origin, he worked in a cotton mill at the age of nine and at 14 years of age became a blacksmith's apprentice. In 1863, he was employed by the Glasgow building firm, Laidlaw & Sons and, in 1868, he invested his life savings of just £85 to found his own business. In 1872 he established the Dalmarnock Works and it is recorded that he would rise at five o'clock each morning at his home in Glasgow and be at the Works by six to begin the business of the day.

His career is a success story of Victorian times. He died in 1913 at the age of 74 at Seafield near Ayr, but his engineering firm continued to give employment to many skilled workers and many young graduates received a sound practical training in structural engineering.

In the early years of the 20th century the structural frame, whether of reinforced concrete or steel, began to dominate architectural form and numerous framed structures were constructed to accommodate civic, commercial, and other buildings. The structural design, detailing, and supervision of the construction of steel and reinforced concrete framed buildings required specialist knowledge and skill. Two structural engineers became well-known names in Glasgow and subsequently acquired a national reputation.

Tom Harley-Haddow, OBE founded his own practice as a consulting structural engineer in 1950 specialising in structures for buildings. He was responsible for much innovation in timber, brickwork, steel and concrete and was a founder member of the Agrément Board. Tom had creative talents beyond his chosen specialisation and after lecturing in structures at the Edinburgh School of Architecture, between 1949 to 1959, qualified as an architect in 1960. He became part of an elite group who combined the creative skills of architecture with those of engineering.

William A. Fairhurst was born in Cheshire, the son of a Midland Railway office worker. His name continues in the public domain as a structural engineering consultancy in Glasgow. At the age of 14 he attended classes at Salford Technical College and subsequently at Manchester College of Technology.

In 1930 he applied for the vacancy of chief structural engineer with the Glasgow consultancy, F.A. MacDonald & Partners. Seven years later he was made a partner, and in 1940, at the age of 36, he became the senior partner.

Although eventually achieving international recognition as a bridge engineer, he became interested in high-rise buildings. He was responsible for the design of three high-rise blocks at Castlemilk; four at Gorbals; and six at Royston. In 1966, the construction of the 31-storey flats (which at the time were the highest in Europe) became a landmark to his design abilities.

He had a great interest in chess and was captain of a UK chess team competing in the Olympics. In 1932, he performed the unusual feat of playing 12 chess matches, simultaneously, blindfolded, and won them all.

He became a well-known structural engineer, an adopted son, who brought great credit to the City of Glasgow.

Professor Iain MacLeod of the University of Strathclyde deserves mention in the context of structural engineering since his early research work, still much used, was concerned with the design of buildings and in particular tall buildings. In the 1960s his analytical computer programs were used extensively for the design of the high-rise blocks in Glasgow (see Chapter 9). Professor MacLeod is an innovative thinker and his ideas have often challenged the conventional wisdom. Over many years he has made a significant contribution to a wide range of research topics and in the development of educational concepts which are merging to form a philosophy of prime importance to industry.

He has been very active in educational work within the Institution of Structural Engineers, being vice-president in 1989. Perhaps as a member of the local community he is best known as a skilled piper; a west coast skipper, and a mountaineer.

It is impossible to do justice to everyone in the discipline of structural engineering having a connection with Glasgow. Historically, it is worth noting that a chair in civil engineering was created at Glasgow University by Queen Victoria in 1840. The first head of department, Lewis Dunbar Brodie Gordon was a highly respected consulting engineer, who had also previously studied practical mining at the Freiberg School of Mines. Gordon was succeeded to the chair by W.J.M. Rankine. Rankine was a truly great scientist, engineer and teacher. His manual on civil engineering was published in 1862 and his development of earth-pressure theory formed the basis of design for earth-retaining structures. His great contribution to soil mechanics is recognised by the annual Rankine Lecture of the British Geotechnical Society; a lecture which is recognised internationally to be the most prestigious lecture on soil mechanics and foundation engineering.

In more recent times, Professor Hugh Sutherland of the University of Glasgow, who had studied soil mechanics in the USA, achieved international recognition and acted as a mentor to many who now enjoy recognition as foundation engineers.

He has been involved in the geotechnical aspects of many nuclear power stations, e.g. Sizewell, and this is only one area where his ability 'to penetrate to the heart of the issue' has been internationally recognised. For example he was awarded an Honorary Citizenship of the City of Winnipeg, Canada for work on the stability of clay slopes, and also awarded the Gold Decoration For Outstanding Merit by the University of Agriculture in Krakow.

When the importance of soil mechanics and foundation engineering was being recognised in the early 1950s young enthusiasts would meet with Hugh Sutherland to discuss and advance geotechnical knowledge in Scotland. From these meetings and the enthusiasm generated the Scottish Geotechnical Group was formed, a specialist group which is still active today.

At Strathclyde University another well-known teacher, Professor David MacKinlay contributed to the development of foundation engineering. He undertook research on glacial till deposits upon which much of the City of Glasgow is founded.

Coincidentally, both Professors Sutherland and MacKinlay were educated at Allan Glen's School and both served as Presidents of the Former Pupils Association. Both also served as chairman of the Glasgow and West of Scotland Branch of the Institution.

Another distinguished chairman of this Association is Dr. Sam Thorburn, OBE who has also contributed greatly to foundation engineering. Sam Thorburn became involved in this specialisation early in his career while working within the steelworks of Colvilles Limited. In 1966 he founded his own general consultancy practice. His interest in understanding and monitoring the behaviour of buildings in service resulted in him becoming a leading expert on the interaction between buildings and their foundations, known as soil-structure interaction. He was elected president of the Institution of Structural Engineers for the session 1997/98 and has continued the Scottish tradition of passing on knowledge as a visiting Professor at the University of Strathclyde; a position he has occupied since 1985.

The varied and often difficult ground conditions on which Glasgow is founded enabled many great foundation engineers to develop their skills. The impetus given by Rankine, Sutherland and MacKinlay and many others to the development of soil mechanics and foundation engineering in Glasgow continues to this day. Sam Thorburn is still active, respected for his contribution to foundation engineering and is recognised as an international authority.

Professor Alan McGown, CBE is an international expert on geotextiles and membranes. He is a graduate of the University of Strathclyde and has had a distinguished career in soil mechanics and foundation engineering. He has been responsible for the introduction of a number of fundamental changes in teaching within his discipline. He has been involved with major industrial companies in the development of materials and products within the construction industry. His success is due not only to a keen intellect but his bubbling enthusiasm, energy, and commitment to his chosen career.

As Glasgow declines from its great industrial past, its importance as a centre of learning continues. Founded in the 15th century and still flourishing today, education built upon a sound foundation has endured and continues to form the basis for the future.

The various engineering disciplines are fundamental to our modern society. Despite the tremendous changes that Glasgow has undergone, the process of learning from experience continues and enables the city to flourish and develop well into the next millennium.